Praise for *Less Talk, More Action*

Bold, brilliant, and deeply practical! Through humility, curiosity, and compassion, Apsey and Freeland empower educators in all roles to turn reflection into results. This is a tactical guide to naming challenges, taking action, and creating real impact. Essential reading!
—**Lainie Rowell,** bestselling author, award-winning educator, and international keynote speaker

Allyson and Emily's *Less Talk, More Action* is an authentic, user-friendly guide for educators and leaders designed to support and transform schools. This book demystifies Action Research, inspiring us to improve our practices and, most importantly, student learning. It provides straightforward steps and approaches for implementing inquiry-based, collaborative actions focused on initiatives that truly make a difference.

As a veteran educator and leader, I have encountered many teachers and leaders seeking to improve their practice and better support students. This guide is for educators at all levels and in all stages of their careers. Whether you are a new teacher or leader, in the middle of your career, or a master educator still seeking to refine your craft, this is the educational improvement book for you. It will help you focus on what matters (and works) the most.
—**Shanna Spickard,** executive director of the Michigan Elementary and Middle School Principals Association (MEMSPA)

Less Talk, More Action is a gift to educators. Allyson Apsey and Emily Freeland offer a clear, hopeful, and practical road map for change rooted in the wisdom of those closest to students—teachers. Their call to replace buy-in with try-in, to embrace reflection paired with action, and to build trust and collective efficacy resonates deeply with my own beliefs about how schools transform. This book empowers educators to lead with curiosity, courage, and hope. It's exactly what our schools need right now.
—**Elena Aguilar,** author

In *Less Talk, More Action*, Apsey and Freeland do an excellent job of providing examples of how staff can not only solve problems they are facing in their classrooms but, more importantly, identify and find problems that are meaningful to them. Defaulting to school communities as the experts of their context, the authors provide actionable ideas that empower staff to define and find their own solutions. When educators are acknowledged as experts, it will always lead to the most meaningful learning in school communities. The authors do a wonderful job of providing guidance in the book while ensuring individual and community ownership of the problems and ultimately the solutions they can create.
 —**George Couros,** innovative learning and leadership consultant, author, and adjunct instructor

Schools don't need another initiative; they need a process that works, and that's exactly what this book delivers. *Less Talk, More Action* puts the power of improvement back into the hands of educators, showing leaders how to create cultures of curiosity, risk-taking, and results. Apsey and Freeland cut through theory and provide a road map for sustainable change filled with high-impact, actionable steps that move the needle in schools and districts. Readers will walk away with practical strategies to identify the right challenges, elevate teacher voice, and turn reflection into measurable impact.
 —**Thomas C. Murray,** author and director of innovation at Future Ready Schools, Washington, DC

Less Talk, More Action delivers a practical framework that transforms how educators approach professional growth and school improvement. Apsey and Freeland bridge the gap between research and reality, giving teachers and leaders concrete tools to drive meaningful change. For educators seeking to build collective efficacy, this book provides both the "why" and the "how" of transformative practice—a road map where curiosity drives improvement and every educator becomes a researcher of their impact.
 —**Dr. Jenni Donohoo,** author and educational consultant

Less Talk, More Action guides us like a reliable school improvement GPS! Allyson Apsey and Emily Freeland clarify why the Action Research process is an essential trip to take. Along the journey they guide us toward the best routes, based on both quantitative and qualitative research; their own real-life stories from schools help us navigate the detours and potholes. The authors say, "Use the results to tell the story of learning." They remind us of the power of Action Research for leaders, teams, and students all engaging in inquiry, reflection, and growth together.

—**Polly Patrick,** international educational consultant, author, and teacher

Less Talk, More Action isn't just another educational book. It is a lived story that details how to create real improvement in your school through a proven process. The authors share a wealth of experience along with stories that educators and leaders can relate to, making it both practical and inspirational. Allyson and Emily provide clear examples and actionable steps to help teams get started on their own journey with Action Research.

The best gift readers will find in this book is the way Allyson and Emily encourage the use of voice and choice, not just for teachers but for students to be a part of the improvement process through metacognition and ownership of their learning. By focusing on one of the most underutilized levers of improvement, the authors remind us that real change happens when students are not only engaged in the process but also trusted to help lead it.

—**Ann McCarty Perez,** author, leader, and director of professional learning

What makes this book different? It is focused on you, the reader. This is not the work of philosophers far removed from the classroom, but of experienced educators who have seen firsthand what relevant Action Research means for students, teaching professionals, and administrators. If you are expecting complicated formulas and five-year plans, this book is not for you. But if you want practical solutions that are directly relevant to your students, your staff, and your community, then read on. With good humor, wit, and thoughtful insights, Apsey and Freeland will reward you with what real research looks like—high impact on students and deep rewards for teachers and leaders. This is a book worthy of study for teachers, administrators, and aspiring educators. It might even persuade you to remain in or join our profession.

—**Douglas Reeves,** author

Common sense is not always common practice. In *Less Talk, More Action*, Apsey and Freeland set the stage for "try-in, not buy-in." Now more than ever, teachers and leaders must embrace learning from one another. There's no need to reinvent the wheel. Instead, let's replicate leadership and teaching strategies that get results. The authors invite readers to teach and lead like scientists so that everyone benefits. This practical resource can be read today and implemented tomorrow.

—**Lisa Almeida,** chief executive officer of Creative Leadership Solutions

Less Talk, More Action

Less Talk, More Action

A Guide to Transforming Schools Through Action Research

Allyson
APSEY

Emily
FREELAND

Less Talk, More Action
© 2025 Allyson Apsey and Emily Freeland

All rights reserved. No part of this publication may be reproduced in any form or by any electronic or mechanical means, including information storage and retrieval systems, without permission in writing by the publisher, except by a reviewer who may quote brief passages in a review. For information regarding permission, contact the publisher at books@daveburgessconsulting.com.

> This book is available at special discounts when purchased in quantity for educational purposes or for use as premiums, promotions, or fundraisers. For inquiries and details, contact the publisher at books@daveburgessconsulting.com.

Published by Dave Burgess Consulting, Inc.
Vancouver, WA
DaveBurgessConsulting.com

Paperback ISBN: 978-1-968898-04-5
Ebook ISBN: 978-1-968898-05-2

Cover and interior design by Liz Schreiter
Edited and produced by Reading List Editorial
ReadingListEditorial.com

For every educator who has ever left a meeting thinking, "We just talked in circles." May this book remind you that even the smallest step forward is worth more than the longest conversation. Take that step because your actions have the power to change lives.

Contents

Introduction: What Is Action Research and How Does It Support Teaching and Learning? 1

Section 1: Setting the Stage for Action Research — 11

Chapter 1: Try-In, Not Buy-In 13

Chapter 2: Innovation Through Action Research 21

Section 2: From Challenge to Change — 29

Chapter 3: Finding the Right Challenge 30

Chapter 4: Action Research for School Improvement 37

Chapter 5: Narrow the Focus: From Inventory to Impact 45

Section 3: Turning Insight into Action — 53

Chapter 6: Taking Action with the Right Practices 55

Chapter 7: Leveraging What Works 61

Section 4: From Data to Impact — 71

Chapter 8: Results: The Story in the Data 73

Chapter 9: Sharing Impact: Telling the Right Story 81

Section 5: Building Collective Efficacy Through Action Research — 87

Chapter 10: Leading Through Action Research 89

Chapter 11: Action Research for High-Performing Teams 97

Chapter 12: Empowering Student Learners Through Action Research 107

Conclusion: Collective Hope: When We Believe in Each Other, Everything Changes 119

Endnotes 122

Acknowledgments 125

About Allyson Apsey and Emily Freeland 126

More from Dave Burgess Consulting, Inc. 130

Introduction

What Is Action Research and How Does It Support Teaching and Learning?

One of our colleagues loves to quote the Farmers Insurance line: "We know a thing or two because we've seen a thing or two." That rings true for both of us. With decades of experience as teachers, principals, district, and state-level leaders, we bring a wide range of perspectives, Emily from high school science, Allyson from elementary and middle school ELA and social studies. Together, we cover the full K–12 spectrum and now support schools and districts nationwide with coaching and professional learning.

We celebrate the progress we see when educators collaborate and act with purpose; and we also hear the frustration of those stuck in endless conversations without change. That's why we wrote this book: because it's time for less talk and more action. Not just any action, but the kind that gets real results.

We've always believed that some of life's most important lessons are tucked between the pages of children's books. One beautifully boxed set by Kobi Yamada especially caught our attention. Its titles ask: *What Do You Do with a Problem? What Do You Do with an Idea? What Do You Do with a Chance?*

Beginning with book one, *What Do You Do with a Problem?*, we are introduced to a character who is initially overwhelmed by a problem and unsure what to do.[1] The more he ruminates on the problem that is following him around, the bigger the problem seems to get. As educators, we can relate. We often face persistent instructional challenges or student learning gaps, and the struggle to find the right solution can make those problems feel overwhelming.

As the character continues on through the day, he hits a turning point. We see him realize that the problem he's facing might actually hold an opportunity. This simple reframing changes his whole way of thinking about his problem.

We next see the character in *What Do You Do with an Idea?* as he stumbles upon an idea.[2] Though his first inclination is to ignore the idea and brush it away, his idea stays with him. He worries what others might think of his idea and feels very protective of it, but he still nurtures and gives his idea more attention. As he does, his idea grows along with his curiosity. In the end, he recognizes that even a simple idea can create significant change.

In the last book, *What Do You Do with a Chance?*, the character allows his first chance to slip away, and when he stumbles encountering his second chance, he decides it may be safer to let other chances go by.[3] Better to avoid embarrassment and fear. As he continues to avoid future chances, he begins to realize that the chances are coming less frequently. Regret sets in when he thinks there may be no more chances. When the next chance appears, he resolves to be brave and seize it, and with that comes a new freedom and new possibilities.

These simple questions are the very ones teachers wrestle with every day. As we dug deeper into Yamada's books, we began to see how each one mirrors an aspect of the Action Research process, which we'll introduce you to in this book. Together, these sweet stories offer a powerful metaphor for the cycle of inquiry, growth, and impact that fuels real change in classrooms and schools.

Taken together, Yamada's books lead us on a journey that follows the cycle of Action Research.

1. **Challenge**: Recognize the problem and name it.

2. **Practice**: Explore and test ideas with intentional action.
3. **Results**: Take a chance on change, analyze the outcomes, and tell the story of what you learned.

Challenges in the classroom, just like in *What Do You Do with a Problem?*, are invitations for inquiry, not obstacles to avoid. There is risk and vulnerability in testing new strategies with students, but also creativity and hope. We may be afraid our idea is the wrong idea, but our idea might also lead to great change. When given attention and time, ideas can grow, just as instructional practices can evolve to meet specific student needs when we use them with intention and include reflection.

Action Research invites us to seize an opportunity—a chance—to reflect on outcomes and make authentic change. Taking a chance, like acting on data, adjusting practices, and sharing results, can be transformative. It allows us to move from only seeing the challenge to embracing possibilities. Chances, when they come, may not be wrapped in comfort, but we should be ready for them, because the next chance just might be the one that changes everything for our students.

Think about your classroom or school. How often are you encouraged to identify and solve the learning challenges your students face? To think differently about your instructional practices? To take meaningful risks without fear? If that hasn't happened lately, we invite you to join us on a new kind of learning journey, one built around a simple but powerful process. It's called Action Research, and it gives us, as educators, a way to turn our reflections into results.

What Is Action Research?

Action Research is a systematic process of identifying a challenge, taking action to address it, and reflecting on the results all at the same time. Unlike clinical research, there's no control group. In education, all students are given the opportunity to benefit from the practices an instructor opts to implement. We compare what we see before the practice was implemented to what happens after.

Action research is a powerful way for us to take charge of our own learning and create meaningful change in our classrooms. At its core, it's about being curious, experimenting with a new method, and learning from the results. What makes Action Research effective, practical, and impactful?

1. **Focused on Real Problems:** It begins with a meaningful question or challenge. Something that matters to you, your students, or your school.
2. **Educator-led:** *WE* lead the process, not outside experts, because we know our students best.
3. **Action-Based:** We don't just think about the problem, we try out ideas, strategies, or tools to make things better.
4. **Reflective:** Throughout the process, we reflect on what's working, what's not, and what we are learning.
5. **Grounded in Evidence:** We collect and use data, like test scores, student feedback, or observations, to see what's making a difference.
6. **Cyclical:** It's not just one and done. We keep learning, adjusting, and improving over time.
7. **Collaborative:** Action Research often happens in teams or learning communities, where we learn and grow together.
8. **Fits Our Context:** It's not one-size-fits-all. We design it to meet the specific needs of our students and school.

Action Research is immediate. It's flexible. It's personal. And it provides concrete evidence of impact, evidence we can see, feel, and share. It is what happens when educators get curious and focus that curiosity. Action Research starts with a question. Maybe some part of new learning is not quite clicking with your students, or maybe you notice a gap between what you hoped would happen as a result of your teaching and what's really going on. Instead of feeling stuck or overwhelmed, you lean in and wonder. You think, "What if I tried something different?"

That simple move of trying something new starts the cycle of Action Research. It begins the process of looking closely at our own practice, not to critique it but to learn from it. We identify a challenge, try a new strategy, and reflect on what happened. We gather data, but more than that, we gather insight. We listen to students, we observe shifts, and we celebrate the small gains that point to real growth. It's not about getting it perfect. It's about being purposeful. Action Research is how we become the educators our students need by being learners and risk-takers ourselves. And the best part? You don't need permission to start. You just need the courage to care, the curiosity to question, and the belief that change is possible, one thoughtful action at a time.

Why Action Research? Why Now?

One constant in our classrooms is complexity. Students are walking through our doors with more diverse needs, and schools are under more pressure to show results. We are being asked to innovate, engage every learner, and help them grow while also identifying learning challenges and accelerating progress for students who are behind grade level. Under these conditions, we can't afford to guess what works. We need real-time insight. We need action rooted in reflection. We need less talk and more action.

Action Research puts the power to improve teaching and learning directly into our hands. It bridges the gap between theory and practice by inviting us to investigate in our own classrooms, test ideas, and track what really moves the needle for students. No more waiting for someone else's answers. No more top-down mandates that don't match the needs of our students or our classrooms. It's time to move away from blindly accepting the findings of others and toward reclaiming our expertise as educators. Action Research empowers us, as teachers and leaders, to become the researchers. It centers our efforts around what actually works for our students—not just in theory but in practice.

So, why now? Action Research is not a new concept. In fact, it dates back to the 1930s, to philosopher and educational reformer John Dewey.[4] It re-emerged in the early 2000s (cue grimaces from anyone who remembers No Child Left Behind). Yet despite its on-again-off-again popularity over the past century or so, it never truly became embedded in school culture. Maybe that's because some educators have viewed it as *one more thing* to do. Maybe it's because many of us don't see ourselves as "researchers." We associate the word *research* with dense reading and studies that don't seem relevant to the needs of our students. Or maybe it's because we've been conditioned to believe that research only comes from outside experts—most of whom haven't stepped foot in a classroom in years. But now is the perfect time for more action, and here's why:

1. **Because the stakes are high.** Learning gaps, engagement issues, and inequities across districts, schools, and classrooms won't fix themselves. Action Research gives us a focused, responsive way to address them.
2. **Because teachers are the experts in their own classrooms.** We don't need outside solutions as much as we need empowered professionals who are trusted to explore, adjust, and lead change.
3. **Because reflection without action leads nowhere, and action without reflection risks repeating mistakes.** Action Research is that just-right balance between trying new things and thinking deeply about what works. It's grounded in everyday classroom experiences, guided by thoughtful reflection, and focused on real change, for students and for us. It helps us make smarter decisions, grow our practice, and meet students' needs in ways that truly make a difference.

Adopting Action Research is not about adding something else to our plate. This *is* the plate—how we grow, adapt, and serve students better. It honors teacher and leader voice, fosters collaboration, and builds a culture where learning never stops. Action Research helps us better understand our students, refine our practices, and unlock the stories behind both success and failure. It helps us stop repeating what doesn't work and start scaling what does.

This isn't just another initiative. It's a movement led by educators who believe that what happens in classrooms matters and that the best answers are often already within our reach.

Let's stop talking about what we *could* do and start doing what we know works.

Less talk, more action. Together.

What You Will Learn in This Book

Section 1: Setting the Stage for Action Research

You'll explore how to cultivate the mindset and conditions necessary for meaningful change. We'll make a shift from buy-in to try-in, to establishing a culture of curiosity and innovation. This section lays the foundation for using Action Research as a tool for transformation—not compliance.

Section 2: From Challenge to Change

You'll learn how to identify the right challenges—the ones that matter most to student learning—and how to use Action Research to move from observation to intentional action. With clarity and focus, school improvement becomes less about reacting and more about responding with purpose.

Section 3: Turning Insight into Action

This section guides you through the heart of the Action Research process: taking intentional steps aligned to the right practices. You'll discover how to select strategies rooted in evidence, leverage what's already working, and begin your cycle of inquiry with momentum and meaning.

Section 4: From Data to Impact

Here, you'll focus on how to gather and interpret meaningful data—not just to measure outcomes, but to deepen learning. You'll also learn how to share your results in ways that build shared knowledge, spark dialogue, and drive continuous improvement.

Section 5: Building Collective Efficacy Through Action Research

Action Research is most powerful when it's done collaboratively. In this final section, you'll explore how leaders, teams, and students can engage in cycles of inquiry that strengthen trust, foster metacognition, and build the collective efficacy that transforms entire school communities.

KEY QUESTIONS TO MOVE FROM TALK INTO ACTION:

1. What challenges are your students facing with their learning and grades?
2. How might the Action Research approach help you address those challenges?
3. What professional learning do you find most meaningful, and how could you incorporate more of that throughout the year?

Section 1

Setting the Stage for Action Research

Section 1 sets the foundation for a different kind of professional growth that begins with the willingness to try. We will expand on the purpose and components of Action Research that were explained in the introduction and dive into strategies and ideas to build a culture of less talk and more action through try-in over buy-in, purposeful experimentation, and leader-supported innovation.

In chapter 1, we will explore the shift from buy-in to try-in, a practical, empowering approach that encourages educators to take action first, build insight through experience, and develop belief over time. Teachers will see how even a small step, like trying one new strategy, can spark meaningful change for students. Leaders will discover how to avoid focusing on developing "buy-in" that sometimes feels like manipulation by creating the kind of culture where trying feels safe, supported, and worth it.

Chapter 2 expands on this mindset by introducing the conditions that make innovation possible. You'll learn how Action Research offers a structured yet flexible process for tackling real challenges, driven by the people who know students best. Teachers will gain tools for inquiry and collaboration, while leaders will learn how to foster trust, model curiosity, and remove barriers that stifle creativity.

This section is about building momentum through action together. Whether you're leading a team or working in a classroom, you'll find practical strategies, reflection tools, and inspiration to help you move from good intentions to lasting impact.

CHAPTER 1

Try-In, Not Buy-In

Every accomplishment starts with a decision to try.

—GAIL DEVERS

Most teachers and administrators have experienced the introduction of new initiatives more times than they can count. You probably have too. You likely remember how it usually starts: a presentation filled with compelling data reveals a problem, followed by theory and research to explain why now is the right time for a new solution. The message is clear: this one new thing will fix the issue, and if everyone does it, it will magically meet the needs of all students. A miracle!

Naturally, this kind of rollout is often met with eye rolls and heavy sighs. Why? Because it rarely takes into account the collective wisdom in the room or the unique complexity of each classroom. Common reactions sound like:

"This is just like that other program we did."

"Here we go again."

"I guess the pendulum has swung back."

At best, leaders spend time and energy trying to get everyone to buy in. At worst, they build systems to monitor compliance. We've been conditioned to believe that effective change can only happen after everyone agrees. But research and experience suggest otherwise. It's not belief that drives behavior, it's behavior that shapes belief.[1]

The idea of buy-in has long been viewed as essential to successful change in schools. Rooted in organizational change theory from the business world, buy-in emerged as a strategy to increase staff motivation and reduce resistance by securing early agreement and support. Leaders have been taught that before any new program or initiative can be implemented effectively, people have to believe in it, emotionally and intellectually. This approach makes sense in theory, right? If people are convinced something will work, they'll be more committed to doing it. Over time, buy-in has become a cornerstone of change management in education, often linked to efforts to build consensus and foster perceived ownership. However, in practice, buy-in has often looked like persuasion campaigns that emphasize presentations, messaging, and compliance over genuine participation. While well-intentioned, this approach can feel like manipulation and overlook the deeper reality that belief doesn't always come first. In contrast, experience is a catalyst.[2]

Our beliefs are built on our experiences, which makes them deeply personal. This is known as "experience bias."[3] We've all learned things "the hard way," gaining understanding through our own challenging or even painful experiences. These moments often stick with us more than lessons we're simply told, and they shape how we see the world. Change initiatives often meet resistance not because we don't care, but because we're asked to shift our beliefs before we've had the chance to shift our experiences. And since those beliefs are tied closely to our professional identity, any challenge to them, even with the best intentions, can feel threatening. Many educators have lived through too many cycles of "the next big thing."

To truly shift beliefs about teaching and learning, we must first create new experiences. The biggest changes don't come from data slides or inspirational speeches. They come from launching a new practice, seeing the results, and feeling the impact. Experience is what builds trust in a new practice and what ultimately changes minds.

The Power of Try-In: A Better Path to Real Change

Instead of aiming for buy-in, what if we asked for try-in? "Try-in" means giving something a fair shot before making a judgment. Shifting from buy-in to try-in moves the focus from *convincing* to *inviting*, and from passive acceptance to active exploration. Rather than saying, "You have to believe in this first," we say, "Let's try this together and see what happens." Yes, innovating can feel risky. What if it doesn't work? Healthy skepticism is okay; it helps us stay grounded. But skepticism shouldn't keep us from giving something a real chance. As Doug Reeves reminds us, we don't need total agreement to begin.[4] We just need a willingness to try.

It's like that old Life cereal commercial from the 1970s. Remember Mikey? (For those of you not even born then, a quick YouTube search will bring it up.) His brothers didn't want to try the cereal, so they said, "Let's get Mikey to try it. He won't like it, he hates everything." But to their surprise, he liked it! So, they gave it a try too. Sometimes, seeing someone else go first is all it takes to ease fear and open us up to new possibilities.[5] Imagine that playing out in schools. Leaders modeling new practices, teachers testing ideas together, and change feeling less like a mandate and more like a shared journey. That's the heart of try-in.

There are several key reasons why try-in is more powerful than buy-in, and each is rooted in action, trust, and meaningful engagement.

1. **It honors teacher expertise.** Educators aren't just implementers, they're innovators. Try-in values our voice and new experiences.
2. **It fosters authentic engagement.** When we help shape the process, we're more likely to commit, not out of compliance, but because we believe in it.
3. **It leads to real results.** Trying something in our own context allows for quicker feedback, learning, and improvement.

4. **It models the mindset we want for students.** Just like students, we need space to explore, reflect, and grow.

In an educational environment that is constantly changing, we don't need more top-down solutions. We need more invitations to learn by doing. Let's stop trying to sell change and start creating space for teachers to experience it. Let's move beyond buy-in and build a culture of try-in. One that leads to shared ownership, continuous growth, and lasting impact. Because once we try and experience what's possible, we just might like it! And more importantly, so might our students.

Embracing the Work (Even with Doubt)

We've met many doubters at the start of this process. Some teachers worry that trying a different technique might lower their success rates. Others fear discovering that a practice they've relied on for years isn't working. That fear is valid. Change always brings a level of vulnerability. But here's what we tell them: Try anyway! Because we can learn just as much from what doesn't work as from what does. Growth doesn't require certainty; it requires courage. As Brené Brown reminds us, "Vulnerability is the birthplace of innovation, creativity, and change."[6] Being willing to step into something unfamiliar, even with doubt, is often what opens the door to real learning and transformation.

And here's the truth: we're not meant to try alone. Trying in isolation can feel overwhelming, but when we build a culture where everyone is learning together, vulnerability becomes strength. It shifts the question from "What if this doesn't work?" to "What might be possible if we did this together?" When we create safe spaces for experimentation, mistakes become data, not failures. They become stepping-stones to insight, clarity, and confidence.

When we first introduce Action Research to a school or district, we're often greeted with hesitancy. Teachers, understandably, ask questions:

- What is this new thing we're expected to do?
- When will we find time for it?
- How long before this, too, disappears?

And we get it. We were those teachers too.

But by the end of our work together, the shift is undeniable. At the start of the year in one high school, we kicked off a grading-focused Action Research journey that was met with groans and grumbles. Teachers even jokingly apologized to each other for having to attend. By the end of the first day together, something beautiful happened. They began to share ideas, see see opportunities opportunities, and believe in their own power to make positive changes for students. As they explored real challenges, tested new strategies, and saw the results with their students, the mood became more positive and excited each month because of the changes they were experiencing. The teachers completed their Action Research projects by the end of the first semester and already knew how they wanted to adjust the practices for even better results in the second semester.

In a feedback survey, one teacher wrote, "This was the most meaningful PD I've had in 17 years." She wasn't just learning, she was doing, and she could see the impact immediately. She even compiled a list of adjustments she wanted to make the following year. The meaning she found through Action Research, combined with the collaboration and support of her colleagues, reignited her excitement for teaching and renewed her belief in herself.

Trying something new, especially in front of students and peers, can feel risky. But action, even imperfect action, creates clarity. In the words of Doug Reeves, "People don't believe what's written in PowerPoints—they believe what they see with their own eyes."[7] It's not the theory or the presentation that builds confidence; it's the experience of seeing something work with our own students that shifts beliefs and builds trust.

When Allyson works with principals, she often shares one of her favorite go-to ideas for staff meetings. It requires almost no prep, works at any point in the school year, and always sparks connection and energy. It's called "Pass It On," and it taps into the collective creativity and expertise already in your building. The idea is simple: teachers bring the best new thing they've tried in their classrooms, whether it's a classroom management trick, a clever organizational system, or an instructional strategy. Then, each staff member chooses one new idea to try in their own classroom, creating a ripple effect of great practice across the school.

"Pass It On!": A Try-In Staff Meeting

Purpose: Celebrate innovation, build collective efficacy, and spread what's working—one small strategy at a time.

How It Works:

Step 1: Set the Stage: Invite each teacher to bring one "bright spot" from their classroom this year, something new they tried that made a positive difference. It can be big or small: a clever classroom routine, a tech tip, a strategy for engagement, or a fresh way to organize materials.

Step 2: Share the Wins: In small groups or stations, each teacher shares their idea briefly (1–2 minutes). You can use a "round robin" format or set up table rotations to keep the energy moving.

Step 3: Capture the Gold: As they listen, teachers jot down the ideas they're most excited to try using a simple recording sheet or sticky notes.

Step 4: Choose One to Try-In: Each teacher picks one new idea to implement in their classroom over the next week or two. Emphasize that this is not about perfection, it's about curiosity and trying something new.

Step 5: Follow Up and Celebrate: Set a plan and a date for a brief follow-up, via email, exit ticket, or at the next staff meeting, where teachers can share how their "try-in" went and what they noticed.

Allyson has seen this idea come to life in different ways, depending on the culture and comfort level of each school. In one building where teachers enjoyed using slides, each person added a slide describing their idea with a photo or short explanation. The result was a shared slideshow full of practical, ready-to-use strategies that staff could revisit anytime. In another school, they recorded the one-to-two-minute share-outs on video so teachers could reflect later in the year or use them to spark ideas in the future. That school even incorporated the videos into their new teacher induction process and found that new staff loved watching them, not just to gather helpful ideas, but to get a glimpse into the expertise of their colleagues. No matter the format, what matters most is creating a space where educators feel valued, celebrated, and energized by one another's success. These small moments of sharing can grow into a culture of collaboration where great ideas don't stay in one classroom and where teachers are willing to try new things.

Theodore Roosevelt said it best: "In any moment of decision, the best thing you can do is the right thing, the next best thing is the wrong thing, and the worst thing you can do is nothing." Inaction keeps us stuck. But action, even with uncertainty, moves us forward. Trying is not just about being fearless. It's about being willing. And that willingness, practiced together, is where meaningful change begins.

KEY QUESTIONS TO MOVE FROM TALK INTO ACTION

1. What's one small practice you've seen or heard about that you're willing to try-in with your students?
2. How might your school or team make it easier and safer for educators to try first, reflect second, and believe through experience?
3. Who can you invite to try-in with you, so you're not doing this work alone?

CHAPTER 2

Innovation Through Action Research

> *Research is formalized curiosity. It is poking and prying with a purpose.*
>
> —ZORA NEALE HURSTON

Whether listening to someone share about a casserole they made or a new car they bought, people always seem to have questions. What are the ingredients? Can I have the recipe? Where did you buy it? Do you love it? It is human nature to be curious. We are wired to want to know more, especially when someone is excited about something that worked. It's no different when it comes to hearing colleagues share about new classroom strategies. When a teacher is enthusiastic when talking about a student breakthrough, others lean in. We lean in not just because we are professionals, but because we are also problem-solvers. We want to know. What did you try? What made the difference? Could that work for my students too?

One of Emily's favorite questions to ask when teachers share their progress with new practices is, "What surprised you the most?" The answers are always revealing. Frequent responses include, "We achieved this improvement with such a simple change," and "It worked, and students actually did better." That sense of surprise and pride signals something important. Innovation doesn't always mean doing more.

Sometimes it means trying something small yet meaningful and then learning from it.

One particularly powerful response came at a recent exhibition of learning. "I am now a believer in Action Research!" This exclamation came from an instructional coach who partnered with the guidance counselor in implementing empathy lessons to address a grade level of students who were treating each other disrespectfully. Emily asked her to share more, and she described how teachers observed noticeable changes in student behavior in just two weeks. After they had planned and delivered their lesson during advisory periods, all grade-level teachers included the skills that were highlighted during those lessons in their daily classroom operations. As a result of their collective efforts, they saw students interacting with greater kindness and respect, not only in classrooms but in hallways too. "It was easy to implement," she said, "and it was so satisfying to see the results." When Emily asked, "What made you want to do the Action Research project, and what made you successful?" the coach paused, then reflected. "It was having the choice to focus on something that mattered to me, and the support of school and district leaders who encouraged me to try something different."

That response says everything. Innovation through Action Research requires ownership, relevance, and support. It doesn't materialize in the form of a mandate. When we are trusted to explore what matters most to us and given space to act on it, we don't need to be coerced or convinced. We lean in. George Couros reminds us that being innovative is not about being the first, it's about being the first to make it work in your context.[1]

That's exactly what this coach did. She didn't wait for the perfect plan. This project exemplifies the power of Action Research: a clear challenge (disrespectful student behavior), a purposeful practice (empathy lessons integrated across settings), and meaningful results (improved student interactions). She started with a meaningful challenge, took action, and made it work for her students.

During another school visit, Allyson and Emily were asked by a superintendent, "What things need to be in place to do this Action Research work?" He went on with "Do we need well-established teacher teams? Are there parameters for what teachers can try? How do you get buy-in? Are all teachers required to participate?" As the questions rolled in, Allyson and Emily found themselves thinking the same thing. Allyson spoke first: "If you really want to set the stage for innovation through Action Research, it starts with leaders."

Leadership sets the tone. Leaders who encourage teachers to try something different, who create an environment that allows for risk-taking, who provide multiple entry points, and who offer the freedom to focus on meaningful, student-centered problems make innovation possible. When professionalism and collaboration are elevated, incredible things happen. When we are trusted as thinkers and empowered as researchers of our own practice, we see tremendous results, not just for students but for the entire school culture.

And perhaps most importantly, as hard as it may be, we must resist the urge to overexplain or spend time in long meetings trying to "sell" ideas. Most of us don't need a pitch. We already care deeply. We are always listening for what works with our students. If we want innovation to flourish in classrooms and schools, then like the Nike slogan says, just do it. Start small. Start with trust. Start by making space to try. Because when we do that, innovation isn't something we demand, it's something we all can embrace.

Permission to Experiment

Before innovation can thrive in schools, something foundational must be in place—psychological safety. We must feel safe to explore, test ideas, and learn from mistakes without fear of judgment or punishment. Yet in many schools, the fear of doing something wrong, disappointing a leader, or stepping outside unspoken norms silently stifles creativity and innovation. Even the most well-intentioned educator can find themselves playing it safe, not because they lack ideas, but because they lack permission.

Imagine being a first-year teacher struggling with classroom management. You've run out of ideas, so you seek help from experienced colleagues. One veteran teacher tells you it's acceptable to keep students in from recess or assemblies to complete missed work caused by off-task behavior. You try it. The first time you do, the principal notices your absence and comes to your classroom, letting you know you're expected at the assembly. It feels like a reprimand. The sick feeling in your stomach lingers for days and resurfaces every time you cross paths with the principal. Trust with your colleagues feels shaky, and from that moment on, you're hesitant to try anything new without your administrator's explicit approval. Scenarios like this aren't as rare as we'd hope, and they serve as a reminder that fear can be both motivating and discouraging.

As Timothy Clark states in *The 4 Stages of Psychological Safety*, "The presence of fear in an organization is the first sign of weak leadership."[2] Weak leaders emphasize compliance, they micromanage, and they rely on positional power. These behaviors create environments where fear thrives. In contrast, strong leaders know that fear stifles learning and innovation. They create space for new ideas, value collaboration, and treat mistakes as opportunities to grow. These leaders build trust, and with trust comes the courage to take risks.

We've all heard the saying "Ask forgiveness, not permission." To risk takers, it's freeing. It's a means to disregard perceived boundaries. They feel more comfortable forging ahead with new ideas and accept that there is always the possibility of an "I'm sorry" at the end of the road. But not everyone feels that freedom.

To rule followers, "Ask forgiveness, not permission" is anxiety inducing and highlights boundaries. For many, the fear of disappointing leaders or appearing out of line leads to paralysis. Even when we are told to innovate, if the environment doesn't support risk-taking, few of us will act. Simply stating, "It's okay to try something new" isn't enough. True permission only exists when the culture embraces mistakes as learning, and failure as part of growth. Without trust, innovation can't take root. Strong leaders foster this trust by creating an environment where everyone feels included, safe to learn, safe to contribute, and safe to challenge the status quo, all without fear of embarrassment, punishment, or marginalization.[3]

Innovation happens when teachers can contribute solutions that challenge the status quo without fear of reprimand. When extending permission to experiment with practices, strong leaders understand that mistakes will be made as part of the learning. In one school we supported, the leadership team offered both a mandate and permission.

The mandate: Everyone would engage in professional learning, either through reading to learn more about Action Research or through participation with their own Action Research project.

The permission: Teachers could choose how they engaged, what they explored, and which practices they implemented with their students.

Because these leaders had already built a foundation of trust, their teachers embraced the opportunity, with many choosing to participate in an Action Research project as their path forward. The permission extended wasn't just verbal, it was embedded in a culture that supported ownership, exploration, and risk-taking. Teachers were given the freedom to decide how they would engage, what they would explore, and which practices they would implement to meet the unique needs of their students. This is the essence of what Sir Ken Robinson describes when he says, "Leadership is not about commanding control, it's about climate control. If you set different boundaries in schools and give people permission to try new things, they will."[4] These leaders didn't dictate innovation. They created the conditions for it to grow through deliberate action steps:

- Modeling curiosity by asking reflective questions in team meetings

- Publicly recognizing small wins and failed attempts as part of growth
- Providing time and structures for teachers to test and reflect on new practices
- Setting clear boundaries (what's nonnegotiable) and generous freedoms (what's open for innovation)
- Inviting teams to document and share the challenge → practice → results cycle

Valuing Inside-Out Change

Each year, schools and districts make decisions about the initiatives they will implement and support. Sometimes money is plentiful, depending on the distribution of grants and government funds. But most of the time, there is a struggle to find the funds needed to provide for professional learning and teacher support. Having to meet the same expectations without additional resources heightens the need to prioritize where we focus our efforts.

One of the greatest resources a school has is the collective expertise of their own teachers. While outside perspectives can offer valuable insights, we often overlook the deep knowledge already within our walls. One of our favorite parts of this work is helping teachers uncover what their students truly need and recognizing the powerful practices already making a difference in their classrooms. What could be more powerful than the learning that comes when teams of teachers collaborate around common student needs? When data from our own students is used to identify specific challenges in learning? When practices are utilized across classrooms and evaluated for their effectiveness?

We've seen this happen when teacher teams ask focused questions, test out small changes, and share results, not just with leadership, but with one another. For example, a sixth-grade math team identified a challenge: students struggled with fractions. They tested a practice:

visual fraction models across lessons. The result: increased student confidence and improved assessment scores.

A group of high school teachers faced a challenge of their own: literacy gaps across subjects. They embedded practices like structured reading protocols. The result: deeper content understanding and improved classroom discussions. These examples reflect the kind of change that isn't dependent on the next big program. It begins with what's already working and builds from there.

Schools will always face funding shortages. There will never be enough time to do everything that we want and need to do. But when we can focus on people, not products or programs, we leverage our most important resources. Practices don't cost us more money. We have all that is needed to elevate and increase the impact we can have on student learning.

It is when we are encouraged, receive permission to try new things, and collaborate around the positive results we get with our own students that momentum builds. The most effective practices grow from within. This allows for change to grow from the inside out.[5] And when that happens, the changes are meaningful, and more importantly, they last. When we ground innovation in real student needs, implement targeted practices, and measure our impact, we move from hope to evidence. Challenge. Practice. Results. This is the rhythm of Action Research and the foundation of lasting improvement.

KEY QUESTIONS TO MOVE FROM TALK INTO ACTION

1. What has surprised you most about a new strategy you've implemented or heard about from a colleague?
2. What conditions in your school or classroom make it feel safe or unsafe to try something different?
3. How can we use what's already working in our classrooms to spark collaborative, teacher-led improvement efforts?

Section 2

From Challenge to Change

We all recognize that school improvement can feel overwhelming. There are so many challenges to address. So many plans to write. So many initiatives are already in motion. But what if we could clear the clutter, quiet the noise, and focus on what really matters for our students?

This section is all about doing just that.

For teachers, these chapters offer permission to slow down, look closely at what your students truly need, and take thoughtful steps forward. You'll find practical guidance to help you choose a meaningful challenge, implement a strategy that fits your classroom, and use Action Research to see real results, without waiting for a state test to tell you how you're doing.

For leaders, you'll discover how to turn your school improvement plan into something that actually improves your school. You'll learn how to align team efforts with big-picture goals, weed out what's not working, and support your staff in doing fewer things better.

Across these three chapters you'll find stories, tools, and strategies that bring clarity, spark curiosity, and build momentum. School improvement is not about doing more, it's about doing what matters most, together.

CHAPTER 3

Finding the Right Challenge

> *In the middle of every difficulty lies opportunity.*
>
> —ALBERT EINSTEIN

Taking an honest and open look at the difficulties your students are experiencing is actually the easy part. When asked what obstacles our students are facing, most of us can rattle off a lengthy list. It's selecting just one issue to focus on that's difficult. How do we choose the area of need that will best support student achievement? Whether you are embarking on Action Research alone or with a team, it is important to consider these two questions:

- What is interfering with student learning the most?
- How much control do I have over this challenge?

When answering the first question, it's essential to look beyond surface-level issues and dig into root causes. The goal is to identify a challenge that, if addressed, could create a ripple effect by removing barriers, improving instruction, and ultimately accelerating student success. By focusing efforts on what matters most, we can ensure that the time and professional development we invest in Action Research leads to meaningful, lasting change.

Examples of responses to "What is interfering with student learning the most?" might include:

- A foundational skill gap, for example, students struggling with subtraction with regrouping, which hinders their ability to grasp long division.
- A deficit in executive functioning skills, such as difficulty breaking a large task into manageable steps, leading to challenges with completing a research project.
- A lack of assessment-readiness strategies, such as not knowing how to approach multiple-choice questions that require selecting more than one correct answer.

Here is how this process played out at one school that cited student attendance as the biggest hurdle to student success. The conversation shifted when the teachers considered the second question: How much control did they have over student attendance? This was a continuation high school where many students were struggling to attend because of a variety of factors. Some had to work to survive, and some had to care for siblings or their own children. The teachers realized that while they could influence student attendance, they couldn't control it. So they dug deeper into the data to find out what was truly standing in the way of learning. What they uncovered was surprising: many students were showing up every day yet still failing. As the team talked through the problem, the answer became clear. These students weren't struggling because they couldn't do the work; they simply weren't turning it in. With that insight, the teachers created a plan to build in weekly catch-up time. Just fifteen minutes was enough to make a powerful difference, helping students follow through and transform effort into success.

Selecting a Challenge Can Be Daunting

Once in a while we work with a teacher or two who really struggle with the idea of Action Research because it can be hard to wrap our minds around research that does not have a control group and can be adjusted mid-experiment. We have to shake off the traditional idea of a research study and embrace the freedom that comes with a focus on challenge, practice, and results. We also have to recognize that sometimes the level of freedom that comes with Action Research is scary because it is overwhelming and does not fit with what teachers normally associate with professional development. We are used to being told what to do and then either embracing an idea, rejecting it, or modifying it. With Action Research, we are not told what to do but instead given autonomy to select our own challenge.

We have worked with schools who gave teachers complete freedom to identify a challenge, and we have worked with schools who asked teachers to select a challenge that was aligned with a particular school-wide focus, a particular set of student achievement data, or student grades. There is power in each of these approaches; it is simply dependent on what the school or district plans to accomplish with the Action Research. So how do you choose a challenge?

- The challenge needs to be meaningful to each teacher.
- The challenge needs to be specific to each teacher's students.
- The challenge needs to be measurable: What data tells you this is a problem? What data will be used to determine the results?

Teachers have strong instincts and intuition shaped by years of experience, and those gut feelings should never be dismissed. But in this case, instinct alone isn't enough. Instead, our hunches should guide us toward which data to explore more closely. When selecting a challenge for an Action Research project, it's crucial that we anchor our decision-making in data.

For example, we worked with a group of teachers who believed that low ELA grades were primarily due to students not turning in the final drafts of their writing projects. Students were doing the in-class work, earning credit along the way, but then failing to submit the final piece and taking a 50 percent—an F—as a result. (Sidenote: This school had already studied fair and accurate grading reform and implemented a minimum 50 percent on assignments to address the mathematical flaws of averaging scores on a 100-point scale.)

When teachers looked more closely at the data, they saw that their instincts were partly right. However, they discovered that the real barrier to student success wasn't just nonsubmission, it was feedback. In addition to reviewing gradebooks, the team conducted student interviews. That's when they uncovered something important: many students weren't turning in their final drafts because they felt overwhelmed by the feedback they'd received. Revising an entire paper felt daunting, and many didn't know where to begin.

So the team turned their attention to their feedback process. They analyzed how they were using rubrics and written comments and realized they needed a more student-friendly approach. They revised the rubric to be clearer and more accessible by removing subjective language, then explicitly taught it to students before sharing feedback. They also began meeting with each student for three quick minutes to walk through the rubric and discuss exactly what to improve. What a brilliant shift! Including student voice helped the team identify the real challenge and sent a clear message to students that their experiences and perspectives were valued.

If the team had stuck with their original assumption that students simply lacked follow-through, they might have implemented practices focused on compliance or external motivation. Instead, they identified the true barrier and responded with a practice that supported student understanding.

Here's how the challenge evolved:

- Initial Challenge: Students are not turning in their final drafts.
- Refined Challenge: Students find the feedback on their rough drafts unclear and overwhelming..
- Targeted Practice: Explicitly teach a student-friendly rubric so expectations are clear. Pair written feedback with a brief individual meeting to help students understand and apply it.

Steps to Selecting Your Challenge

Selecting the right challenge for your Action Research project can lead to results that benefit your students and can also be shared with colleagues to multiply the impact across classrooms and teams. Choosing the right challenge sets the foundation for meaningful inquiry, intentional improvement, and scalable success.

Step 1: Identify a pressing challenge by asking, "What is one thing currently interfering with student success that, if addressed, could make the greatest difference?"

Start by reflecting on patterns you've observed in student learning or engagement. This could stem from assessment data, classroom behavior, or instructional routines. Aim to uncover a key barrier blocking success for a large group of students, with the potential for lasting improvement if solved.

Step 2: Determine if it is a challenge that you have direct control over.

It's tempting to focus on problems outside your sphere of influence, things like district-wide curriculum changes or systemic inequities. While those are valid concerns, effective Action Research focuses on what you can directly influence in your own classroom or team. Think about the instructional strategies, routines, or decisions you and your colleagues can implement and adjust right now.

Step 3: Ensure the challenge is meaningful, specific, and measurable.

A well-defined challenge increases the likelihood of a successful outcome. A meaningful challenge is one that truly matters for student growth and is supported by data, not one that is based on assumptions. A specific challenge is clearly defined, avoiding vague goals or broad ambitions. Rather than stating, "We will improve reading scores," with Action Research, we get specific and focus on what is interfering with student reading achievement the most—do they need to improve comprehension skills? Fluency? Vocabulary? And a measurable challenge is one you can track over time, using data to monitor progress and inform next steps. Ask yourself: How will we know if our actions are working?

The first step in Action Research, choosing the right challenge, is where curiosity meets purpose and where concrete data and our instincts as educators guide us toward what truly matters. When we take the time to identify a challenge that's meaningful, measurable, and within our control, we set ourselves up to make a real difference not just for our students but for ourselves and our teams.

This work isn't about perfection. It's about progress. It's about asking better questions, staying open to what the data tells us, and being brave enough to explore new strategies. Action Research gives us the chance to slow down, reflect, and take intentional steps forward. And when we share our learning with others, the impact extends beyond our own classroom walls.

KEY QUESTIONS TO MOVE FROM TALK INTO ACTION

1. What data sources do you currently rely on to identify student learning challenges, and what might you be overlooking?

2. What student learning challenge are you considering focusing on? How can you refine a broad challenge into a specific, actionable focus that is within your control and meaningful for your students?
3. Who in your school or district might already be having success with a similar challenge, and how might you learn from or replicate their practices?

CHAPTER 4

Action Research for School Improvement

> *Excellence is not a destination; it is a continuous journey that never ends.*
>
> —BRIAN TRACY

At one middle school in the Midwest, student chatter in the hallway included complaints about homework, confusion about learning goals, and struggles to stay motivated. The staff felt it too; something wasn't clicking. Teachers there believed in their students' potential, but the outcomes didn't always reflect it. So, the school tried something different.

Instead of introducing another new program or waiting for answers from outside experts, the leadership team turned inward and launched their own school-wide initiative rooted in Action Research that would address challenges specific to their school. This initiative wouldn't be just for teachers, it would be for the entire school community, including students.

It began with one simple but powerful question: What if curiosity became the engine of our improvement efforts?

Each grade-level Collaborative Learning Team selected a focus question based on patterns they noticed in their classrooms. One seventh-grade team asked, "What happens when we give students more voice in how they show their learning?" Another wondered, "Could reflective journaling improve students' problem-solving in math?"

Teachers gathered data, studied patterns, and refined their strategies. But the shift didn't stop there, because students joined the process too. They learned to ask meaningful questions about their own learning, try new strategies, track their progress, and reflect on what worked.

One student explored how movement breaks affected her focus during reading. Another tracked whether setting daily goals helped him complete assignments more consistently.

Soon, classroom walls were covered with charts, sticky notes, and artifacts of thinking. Conversations shifted from frustration to problem-solving, from "What's wrong?" to "What can we try next?" Over time, student engagement increased, teachers felt more connected, and the entire school culture began to shift. They weren't just solving problems, they were learning how to learn together.

By year's end, the middle school had more than a collection of Action Research projects: it had developed a living, breathing model of school improvement that was collaborative, reflective, and rooted in curiosity. Through Action Research, students and staff alike discovered a new way forward; one that built ownership, sparked metacognition, and made learning visible at every level.

As a result of this momentum, the educators aligned its school improvement plan for the upcoming year around three clear goals: increase student ownership of learning, strengthen formative assessment practices, and deepen collaborative teacher inquiry. Action Research became the vehicle for achieving these goals. Each Collaborative Learning Team built its action plan around data-informed inquiry cycles, ensuring their work aligned with school-wide priorities. The leadership team committed to ongoing support, embedding time for reflection, data analysis, and peer learning throughout the year. Instead of chasing new initiatives, the school chose to refine and scale what was already working. With a shared vision, a clear structure, and the curiosity to keep learning, the school's improvement plan wasn't gathering dust on a shelf. They lived it.

Reclaiming the Purpose of School Improvement

Every school has an acronym for Continuous School Improvement (CSI), whether it's SIP (School Improvement Plan), TIP (Targeted Improvement Plan), or something else.

As we reflect on the success story of the Midwest middle school, it becomes clear that effective school improvement isn't about writing better plans, it's about living them. But too often, school improvement plans become disconnected from the very classrooms they aim to support. Being a school or district that focuses on continually improving is an ideal we all strive for. Unfortunately, CSIs, SIPs, TIPs, etc. have become more about a requirement we need to fulfill rather than focusing on real efforts to change. CSI plans almost always list a reading and math goal, along with one more focused on English language learners, social-emotional learning, or maybe graduation/dropout rates. The goals are written generically to address larger skills like reading comprehension or math computation, or simply to improve math or reading scores on the state assessment.

We often spend hours in meetings reviewing data, writing goals, making lists of activities we will use to address those goals, and wordsmithing each part with educational lingo to check all of the boxes for compliance and monitoring. Allyson and Emily, in planning support for schools, have reviewed school improvement plans ranging anywhere from twenty to a hundred pages. Needless to say, most are hard to read and understand. They also typically fall short of clear actionable steps that can be linked directly to student improvement. Sadly, many sit in their binder on a shelf or on a rarely clicked link on the district website for the bulk of the school year. They are rarely revisited and revised based on measured levels of implementation and changes in data.

Have you ever seen that ad campaign on TV that features "stronger" paper plates? There have been multiple versions over the years, but they all look something like this: A guy is at a picnic filling up his generic paper plate with barbeque and sides. After he has overloaded it with food, he turns to walk away from the table, and the plate collapses, dumping everything all over his white T-shirt.

We are then reminded that if he had just used the "stronger" plate, he could have piled the food as high as he wanted, and there would be no mess.

Let's compare this with what we do in schools. It may seem silly, but stick with us. Through the improvement process, we are often piling one initiative after another on teachers' plates. Try as they might to balance and hold all the new curriculum and tools with all the other things they have to do, their plates can eventually collapse. We seldom stop to consider that just because they can hold more doesn't mean they should.

Imagine the possibilities when we narrow our focus to a few high-leverage initiatives that directly impact student learning. By choosing to go deep rather than wide, schools can create the conditions for meaningful implementation, sustained progress, and measurable improvement. Instead of spreading energy across countless disconnected efforts, educators can concentrate their time and expertise on what works: strengthening practices, deepening understanding, and building momentum that lasts.

Action Research as a Solution

Instead of continuing the cycle of overloaded plans and scattered initiatives, schools need a focused, flexible process that brings clarity and purpose to improvement efforts. That's where Action Research becomes a game-changer. It empowers teachers and leaders to be intentional, identify specific challenges, implement targeted strategies, and study their impact in real time. Through regular cycles of inquiry, reflection, and refinement over the course of the school year, teams make informed decisions grounded in data and professional expertise, and this means no more waiting for end-of-year test scores to tell us what worked. This kind of responsiveness turns improvement into a daily practice, not just a plan on paper. Rather than layering on more initiatives, Action Research helps schools sharpen their focus, build collective efficacy, and drive meaningful, sustainable change from the inside out.

Linking Action Research to School Improvement Goals: A Practical Framework

This chart outlines the steps for linking Action Research to school improvement goals.

1. Identify the School Improvement Goal *Which specific goal will be targeted?*	*Increase reading comprehension in grades 6–8 by 10 percent.*
2. Define the Challenge *What specific instructional or operational issue is affecting progress toward this goal?*	*Seventh-grade students are struggling to analyze nonfiction texts in content-area subjects.*
3. Identify and Implement the Practice *What practice (e.g., instructional change, resource, schedule shift) will be used to address this challenge? Who will implement it and over what time period?*	*Students will use graphic organizers while analyzing nonfiction texts twice weekly for six weeks in all grade 7 classes.*

4. Collect Evidence and Analyze Results *Did the strategy improve outcomes toward the school goal?* *What should be sustained, scaled, or revised?*	*Qualitative and Quantitative* • *Student work samples* • *Classroom assessments or screeners* • *Observation notes* • *Surveys (students, teachers)*
5. Share Findings and Plan Next Steps *How will you share results (presentation, PLC, data display) so that others can engage with the findings?* *What conditions or resources are needed for others to replicate this practice successfully?* *Based on results and student responses, what would you adjust if you repeated this process?*	• *Communicate results to leadership teams and staff* • *Align adjustments with future school improvement actions* • *Use findings to inform professional development or policy decisions*

The specific actions taken at each grade level addressed in the school-wide goal may be different, but the process and intended results are the same: improved reading comprehension. Each grade level is targeting improvements in reading, and they are each identifying the learning challenge that is unique to their students.

Actions for Improvement

During a recent site support visit, Emily found herself in a discussion with the principal about updating their school improvement plan. Because the principal was new to the role and to the school, the plan had been inherited from the previous principal. She wanted Emily's help to evaluate the implementation and revise the goals and action steps for next year. To guide this process, Emily encouraged the principal to start by engaging teacher teams in a collaborative review of the current improvement plan. The goal wasn't just compliance, it was about making the plan meaningful and reflective of real teaching and learning. Together, they designed a reflective protocol that would help teams evaluate what had been implemented, what had impact, and what needed to be adjusted.

The principal used this Reflect and Refocus Protocol with staff.

Reflect and Refocus Protocol

With your grade-level team, read the school improvement goals and strategies. Then reflect using the following prompts:

- What didn't we do that we should have?
- What did we do that we no longer need?
- What did we do that worked and should be scaled up?
- What can we add to target unmet needs?

On Emily's next visit, the principal shared how productive the conversations had been. They had deep discussions about their work, reflected on what they had accomplished, and assessed where they had fallen short. They identified many initiatives listed in the plan they didn't even remember because there was just so much. Most importantly, they had been able to determine as a group where they wanted to take the school next. They were able to take that next step because they had collaboratively examined what was working and what was not.

The path from where we are to where we want to be begins with focus. When we take stock of what's working and what isn't, we gain clarity about our students' needs and our own impact. That clarity allows us to align our efforts with what matters most. Rather than limiting our impact, narrowing our focus deepens it. That's when real, lasting improvement begins to take root.

The best improvement plans lay out a clear path forward by identifying precise student needs and aligning them with targeted teacher and leader actions. With a focused process, we can determine what is truly working for students, amplify those effective practices, and let go of those that fall short. In this chapter, we've explored the tools and the capacity that already exist within our schools. In the next chapter, we'll take a closer look at how schools can audit their existing initiatives and determine where to invest their time, energy, and resources for the greatest impact.

Whether we're scaling excellence or empowering teacher teams to try in through Action Research, meaningful change begins with choosing a focus. That focus lays the foundation for sustained improvement for students, staff, and the entire school community.

KEY QUESTIONS TO MOVE FROM TALK INTO ACTION

1. How might your school or district benefit from using Action Research as a tool for collective improvement, not just individual growth?
2. In what ways can we engage students, teachers, and leaders in a shared process of inquiry and reflection?
3. What systems or structures do we need to put in place to support a culture of curiosity, collaboration, and continuous learning?

CHAPTER 5

Narrow the Focus

From Inventory to Impact

> The essence of strategy is choosing what not to do.
>
> —MICHAEL PORTER

Pause your reading for a moment and pick up your cell phone. Take a moment to scan your phone and count how many apps you've downloaded. Now, identify your top five most-used apps. What makes them so useful or appealing? Next, find five apps you've never used. What do they have in common, and why are they still on your phone?

What does the number of apps on your cell phone have to do with schools and classrooms? Well, the apps on our phones are very much like the programs and initiatives we purchase and utilize in our schools, especially when it comes to school improvement initiatives. With each new year, school and district leaders seek out those things that have the potential for instant impact with students.

Teachers do the same, often spending their own money to use them in their classrooms. The programs, initiatives, and even strategies that are easiest to implement and the ones we simply like best tend to be the ones that are used the most. If we don't like a program or initiative, or if it is hard to use, we're more likely to avoid using it, even when vast resources have been poured into those programs. It's human nature, and the available time we have to plan and implement new things is limited and precious. That's why we need to narrow our focus and home in on where we need to spend our time.

Before we can sharpen our focus, we need to see the full picture. The From Inventory to Impact cycle helps schools examine their current landscape by identifying what they're using, how it's working, and what to prioritize. The goal isn't to do more, it is to do less by focusing on what actually works.

Just as we took an inventory of our phone apps, it is time for us to take an inventory of the programs and initiatives in our districts and schools. The four steps of the From Inventory to Impact cycle provide an excellent lead-up to Action Research because it helps us identify where we need to invest our time and effort, and what initiatives we can leave behind. As we go through each step of the cycle pause your reading to complete the tasks in each step.

FROM INVENTORY TO IMPACT:
A Four-Step Initiative Review Cycle

STEP 1:	STEP 2:	STEP 3:	STEP 4:
List the Initiatives	Determine the Source	Determine the Level of Use	Determine Where to Focus

Step 1: List the initiatives.

Make a list of the programs and initiatives purchased by and/or used in your school. Try not to be alarmed if the list seems long. Long lists are not out of the ordinary. If you are unsure of how to define *initiative*, here's a description that might be helpful: "A planned action or program implemented within a school to address a specific need, improve a system, or achieve a desired outcome." If it is not part of business as usual, consider it an initiative. Be sure to include as many as you can recall, even ones not reflected in the school improvement plan.

Step 2: Determine the source of the program or initiative.

Just like our apps, new programs and initiatives in schools can come from a variety of sources, making it important to understand where they originate. Improvement is a goal at all levels of education, and many different individuals and organizations offer resources to support success.

Now, list the source of each program or initiative. Is it a state-wide, district-wide, school-wide, or grade-level program or initiative? If you are unsure, no worries. Just put what you believe to be most accurate. Also determine the level of requirement. Is it just available as a resource? Is its use highly suggested? Is it required by the district? Is it mandated by the state? We both have experiences with initiatives that were perceived to be required but actually were not. This distinction can be very helpful when deciding to keep or move away from an initiative.

Step 3: Determine the level of use and overlap.

Many schools have overlapping programs that serve similar purposes. They perform the same function, but let's be frank, some of the reports are easier to read, some are much more teacher and student friendly, and some get better results than others. Look at your list: Are any initiatives duplicative or competing? Which ones are used more often, and why? Take note of what's working, what's being used out of obligation, and what's simply not being used at all. Make note of the ones that are duplicates.

Step 4: Determine where to focus.

Now that we've taken stock of our initiatives and programs and looked closely at where they came from, how much they're being used, and what makes each one unique, it's time to ask the most important question: Where do we focus from here? This is our opportunity to be thoughtful and intentional. It's not about doing more, it's about doing what works *best* for our students.

Lean into the practices that are making a real difference and decide which initiatives and programs need to be expanded, which are solid enough to sustain, which may need another look, and which can be discontinued.

The following framework provides a decision-making process to classify any initiative into one of these four categories: Invest, Lead, Evaluate, or Weed. It considers the impact on student results and the implementation level in the school. This framework (adapted from Dr. Douglas Reeves's Implementation Audit model) helps school leaders weed out low-value initiatives and focus on high-impact practices.

High Implementation	
High Impact **INVEST** Maintain & Scale Continue supporting and scaling what works well	**Low Impact** **EVALUATE** Review & Reflect Widespread but underperforming—investigate why
Low Implementation	
High Impact **LEAD** Scale & Support Hidden gems—requires leadership action to grow	**Low Impact** **WEED** Let It Go Low use, low results—it's time to remove

Invest: High impact, high implementation

Continue investing to maintain and scale up this successful practice because this initiative or program is a proven success and is already ingrained in practice. Leaders should maintain and support its ongoing success, continue allocating resources, provide training when needed, and focus on sustaining the impact. This is an area where we can keep on keeping on!

Examples of initiatives to *invest* in:

- A co-teaching model that has improved inclusion practices and student outcomes for learners with IEPs, with consistent implementation across grade levels.
- A school-wide writing rubric and protocol used in every subject area, leading to measurable improvement in student writing performance on local assessments.

Lead: High impact, low implementation

This initiative or program is a hidden opportunity even though utilization is not yet widespread, so leadership involvement to scale up this promising practice is the way to go. To maximize the benefits, leaders must provide professional development, model its use, allocate time for teachers to plan or collaborate, and remove barriers inhibiting implementation.

Examples of initiatives to *lead*:

- A peer-feedback protocol that boosts student metacognition but is only used by a few teachers. PD time can be provided so the teachers can share the effectiveness, and teams can collaborate on when to use the protocol and to plan progress monitoring.
- A restorative practices framework introduced in professional learning but not yet embedded in daily discipline routines.

Evaluate: Low impact, high implementation

This widespread practice needs review to determine next steps because this initiative or program is widespread but is not producing the desired results. Because so many teachers are invested in its use, a thorough review is needed to understand why it isn't working as expected and to determine next steps. By examining data more closely, gathering teacher and student feedback, and considering if the implementation can be improved or if the issue is a misalignment, we can then decide if it is worth additional support or if it should be phased out.

Examples of initiatives to *evaluate*:

- A mandated weekly test-prep block that consumes instructional time but has an unclear effect on state assessment results.
- A digital assessment tool that is used regularly, but teachers report is time-consuming and doesn't provide actionable data.

Weed: Low impact, low implementation

This initiative or program has shown minimal to no benefit and little uptake, so consider discontinuing it and reallocating resources. It's time to have the courage to let it go. Frankly, it probably should have been dropped already. Since it's not widely used and not producing results, it's relatively easy to "weed out" of your school's garden. Dr. Reeves reminds us, "Weeds do not need analyses, lectures, or strategic plans. They need to be pulled out by the roots and discarded."[1] Removing these low-value initiatives and programs frees teachers to focus on what matters most for students. Even if you have to pry them from some teachers' hands or sneak into their classrooms after hours, it's time to let go!

Examples of initiatives to *weed*:

- An online vocabulary program purchased three years ago, used inconsistently across classrooms, with no evidence of impact on reading scores.
- A character education poster campaign that was rolled out school-wide but never integrated into lessons or school culture.

Much time, energy, and resources go toward planning and implementing school improvement initiatives and programs. By using this framework, school leaders and teacher teams can focus on what works best and ensure their energy is devoted to initiatives that truly benefit students. This process helps create a culture of intentional practice by focusing on doing fewer things better.

At the school level, Action Research aligns everyday teaching and leadership practices with specific school improvement goals. Whether the focus is on improving literacy outcomes, promoting inclusive practices, enhancing student engagement, or supporting behavior interventions, Action Research offers a structured yet flexible framework for testing strategies and measuring their impact. It encourages collaboration among educators, builds professional capacity, and supports a shared commitment to continuous growth. When leaders make the focus of school improvement more than just the state assessment, they set the stage for a learning environment where initiatives and programs are grounded in evidence, and improvement is driven by those closest to the students. It's time for less talk and more action when it comes to school improvement plans.

KEY QUESTIONS TO MOVE FROM TALK INTO ACTION

1. Which of your current initiatives are truly moving the needle for student learning, and which ones are just taking up time and resources?
2. What would it look like to narrow your focus and go deeper with fewer, higher-impact practices?
3. How can you make your school improvement process more dynamic and responsive? How can you make it part of your daily practice instead of something that's sitting on a shelf in a binder?

Section 3

Turning Insight into Action

This section is about more than just identifying what's not working, it's about noticing what is, and learning how to make it work for more students. When schools treat success as something to be studied, shared, and scaled, powerful things happen.

For teachers, this section offers tools to help you choose and implement the right practices, ones that match your students' needs, fit your context, and lead to real improvement. You'll learn how to investigate your own data, tap into the strengths of your colleagues, and experiment with confidence, knowing that growth, not perfection, is the goal.

For leaders, this section provides a replicable process for elevating what works across your school or district. You'll learn how to build structures that celebrate teacher expertise, encourage collaboration, and scale effective practices without mandating uniformity. When we create systems for sharing success, we turn isolated excellence into collective growth.

Whether you're exploring a new strategy or leading a school-wide effort, this section helps you focus on what works, and how to make it work for more students, more often, with greater impact.

CHAPTER 6

Taking Action with the Right Practices

Knowing where to focus is powerful. Knowing what to do next is transformational.

—ALLYSON APSEY AND EMILY FREELAND

We all have experienced the letdown of experimenting with a new approach and watching it have little to no impact on student success. We see an idea shared on social media that sounds amazing, but for some reason, it just doesn't work in our classroom. In those moments, it's easy to think the strategy failed. Or worse, that we did. But what if the problem wasn't the practice but the mismatch? In this chapter, we explore how choosing the right practice, one that truly meets the moment, can transform your Action Research journey from trial-and-error to trial-and-growth.

In chapter 3, we shared the story of a team of ELA teachers who thought the problem was simple: students weren't turning in their final writing drafts. But instead of acting on assumptions, they got curious. They listened. And that made all the difference, because they found it wasn't a motivation issue, it was a feedback issue. Students weren't disengaged; they were overwhelmed. With that new understanding, the team chose a different approach. They didn't reach for the easiest or most popular strategy. They matched their practice to the real challenge, and it worked.

That's the heart of this chapter: making that same kind of thoughtful, intentional match in your own work. Because identifying the challenge is only half the equation. The real magic happens when you choose a practice that meets the moment. The right practice is not always the flashiest one, the easiest one, or the most popular one. The right practice is the one that will work for your students, in your context, for their specific challenge.

So, how did that ELA team determine which practice to select?

They understood that some of the best research is completed right in your own school: what works for *your* students and in *your* setting. So, they turned to one of their colleagues who was finding success with students completing their final drafts with positive results. They were all teaching similar students in similar settings, with the same resources and schedules. They knew that what their colleague was doing could be replicated with ease. So, they sat down with her to learn the methods she was using and then implemented them in their own classrooms. They were proud but not surprised that their students experienced the same success as her students.

Each Action Research project is different, and that is the beauty of this work. Sometimes teams may focus on the same challenge but implement different practices to address the challenge, and this is powerful learning also. Chances are that some of the practices will work better than others, and the team can use that information to determine next steps.

Sometimes individual teachers or teams will turn to research-proven practices that they find in a book or other resource. This especially happens if no one on the team is finding success or if an individual teacher is embarking on Action Research on their own. It is okay if no one on your campus or in your district has figured out a formula for success yet for the challenge you have selected; someone out there most likely has a strategy that will work for your students. It is just a matter of doing the work to find the ideas, selecting the best one to meet your students' needs, and then giving it a fair try to see if it works.

Matching the Right Practice to the Challenge

Once you've identified your challenge, don't rush to implement the first solution that comes to mind. Use these intentional steps to select a practice that truly fits:

1. **Clarify the Root of the Challenge:** Go beyond surface-level symptoms. What's really getting in the way of success? Use data, student feedback, and professional judgment to dig deeper.
2. **Define Success:** What would it look like if this challenge were resolved? Be specific about the outcome you're hoping for because this helps guide your choice of strategy.
3. **Explore Practice Options:** Brainstorm a few instructional practices or approaches that could address the challenge. Look within your own school, across your district, or in research-based sources. Prioritize those with a strong track record and alignment to your goals.
4. **Check for Fit**
   - Is the practice doable within your context?
   - Does it align with your team's values and current work?
   - Will it help students meet the goal you've defined?
5. **Select One Practice to Try:** Choose one promising, manageable practice to implement. Less is more. Focus allows for depth, reflection, and real change.
6. **Plan for Implementation:** Decide who will do what, when, and how. Build in time for reflection and progress checks as you move forward.

Learning Forward, Not Failing

Here is your official permission slip to adjust as you go. Allyson once worked with a teacher who, after wrapping up her Action Research cycle, quietly shared, "I think my project failed." She had noticed a persistent pattern in her classroom: many students were falling behind on assignments and struggling to follow through on multi-step projects. After digging into the issue, she realized it wasn't a lack of ability, because her students proved they could do the work. The real challenge was executive functioning: they needed more support to stay organized, monitor their progress, and manage deadlines. So, she designed a thoughtful strategy to conference with students about their academic progress and helped each of them create an action plan for improvement. On paper, it checked all the right boxes: student ownership, goal-setting, individualized support. But as the project wrapped up, she was disappointed. The impact wasn't as big or widespread as she had hoped. Most students participated, but only a few truly seemed to shift their behavior or performance.

Rather than labeling the project a failure, Allyson asked, "What did go well? Did anything shift, even for one student?" That simple question sparked a new perspective. The teacher began to reflect on a few students who had clearly benefited from the conversations, students who rarely spoke up in class but had opened up during conferences, students who followed through on their action plans and showed growth in their next assessment. While the strategy didn't lead to sweeping changes for the whole class, it led to meaningful breakthroughs for a few.

Most powerfully, the teacher realized that the practice she chose wasn't wrong, it just needed adjusting. She noticed that students didn't always know how to translate feedback into next steps. So, she revised her conference format to include sentence starters, visual prompts, and a timeline to guide students in creating their action plans. With that small shift, more students were able to engage in the process meaningfully. The revised version of the practice had a bigger impact because she was willing to reflect and refine instead of giving up.

That's what makes Action Research so powerful. It's not about getting it perfect on the first try. It's about learning in motion, responding to real-time insights, and staying curious about what students need. Sometimes what feels like a failure is actually the beginning of something far more effective.

Students notice when we are paying attention to their needs and trying new things. One student got curious about our presence in the classroom and asked us what we were doing. When we mentioned that we were working with teachers to help improve learning, he lit up and said, "That's cool. Are you, like, figuring out what works better for us?" He went on to say that he'd noticed his teacher trying some new things lately, like helping them break down assignments into smaller steps and checking in more often, and that it actually made school feel less stressful. His simple question was powerful and spot-on. That's exactly what Action Research is: a shared effort to learn what works, for real students, in real classrooms. When students see that we're not just teaching them but learning with them, it builds trust, engagement, and a sense of partnership. They stop being passive recipients of education and start becoming active participants in the learning process.

That brief conversation was a reminder that students watch us closely and they feel the impact of our efforts. When we slow down to learn, reflect, and adjust, they notice. But we also know that time is one of the most precious and limited resources in schools. With full schedules, growing demands, and constant new initiatives, it can feel overwhelming to try something different. That's why the goal isn't to add more to our plates, but to focus our energy on what's most effective. When we invest time in practices that truly meet students' needs, we multiply our impact.

So often in education, we're asked to implement solutions before we've fully understood the problem. Action Research flips that script. The path to real improvement isn't paved with flashy programs or quick fixes, but rather it's built on intentional steps, guided by inquiry, and driven by what our students truly need. When we pause long enough to listen to the challenge, select a thoughtful response, and stay open to adjusting along the way, we're creating a culture of continuous learning. Action Research is about progress. The path forward isn't always straight, and the results may not be immediate. But when we treat every step as an opportunity to learn, refine, and grow, we move closer to a culture where improvement is a shared journey rooted in curiosity, clarity, and care.

KEY QUESTIONS TO MOVE FROM TALK INTO ACTION

1. Have you clearly defined the root cause of your challenge, beyond surface-level symptoms?
2. What practices have the greatest potential to meet this challenge in your context, with your students?
3. How will you quickly and clearly know if the practice you choose is making a difference?

CHAPTER 7

Leveraging What Works

> *The way a child discovers the world constantly replicates the way science began. You start to notice what's around you, and you get very curious about how things work.*
>
> —DAVID CRONENBERG

When we talk with teachers about the idea that success and evidence of what works for students in their context is already happening all around them, we often see a familiar reaction. They pause, look up, and tilt their heads slightly, the way someone does when something really makes them think. You might be doing it right now.

Just like savvy poker players read "tells" at the table, savvy professional learning facilitators do the same in workshops. They watch for the head tilts, the lifted eyes from laptop screens—those subtle signs that something just landed. Teachers are used to hearing about research-based practices, but they don't always realize that some of the most effective instructional strategies might be happening right next door, or even in their own classroom.

Once we have their attention, teachers begin to process the idea that the keys to overcoming student learning challenges are often already present in their school, their teams, or even their own classroom. The first thing we often hear from them is something like: "That makes sense. There are teachers here getting excellent results. But what holds us back from sharing success and learning from each other?"

We love answering a question with a question to provoke deeper thinking, so we turn this one around and ask teachers, "Why do you think that is?" They respond with a myriad of thoughtful answers, all of which make sense.

- We're modest. Sharing our successes might seem like we're bragging.
- We don't see each other teach, so we assume we all do things alike, though we actually do things very differently.
- There is not enough time to collaborate, so our conversations never get that deep.
- No one has asked us to think of successful evidence-based practices that are happening in our own school or district.
- We use data to look for weaknesses; we usually don't analyze causes of success.

When teachers share these honest responses, it becomes clear: it's not that they're unwilling to share their successes, they simply need support when it comes to mindset, opportunity, and systems. We're not used to shining a light on what's working, especially when it feels like bragging or when time is short. But imagine what could happen if we created the space, the permission, and the curiosity to do just that. What if we got just as good at analyzing what is working as we are at diagnosing what's not? That shift from isolation to shared insight might be the most powerful step we can take to move learning forward for every student.

It might seem strange to begin this chapter with a quote from a horror-film maker, but David Cronenberg's observation is apt. We've already talked about the fact that Action Research is all about teaching like a scientist. Just like children noticing the world around them with curiosity, it's time to get curious and notice things around us that are working, rather than solely focusing on the things that aren't.

A Framework for Scaling Success

To truly improve learning at scale, we need more than inspiration, we need a system. In chapter 11, we explore how to shift teams from transactional to transformative. To reach that level of transformation, both beliefs and processes must align to create a foundation for sustainable improvement. The Unlocking Pockets of Excellence cycle is designed to do just that. This five-step process helps schools identify what's working, uncover why it works, and empower others to apply those practices. Grounded in curiosity, collaboration, and continuous reflection, the cycle moves us from isolated wins to collective growth, ensuring that every student benefits from what we already know works.

To put this process into action, we can follow a simple, repeatable cycle that can be used again and again.

Step One: Identify the "Who"
Use evidence to identify pockets of excellence.

Step Five: Reflect on Results
Reflect on what worked and what didn't to define next steps in this continuous cycle.

Unlocking Pockets of Excellence
How to Uncover and Scale Teacher Success

@AllysonApsey

Step Two: Analyze the "What"
Observe the class(es) in action to begin to identify causes of success.

Step Four: Scale the Success
Using teacher leadership and collaboration, empower teachers to try the practices.

Step Three: Discover the "How"
Engage in deep conversations with the teacher(s) to unlock details of successful practices.

www.AllysonApsey.com

In an era when schools are stretched thin and initiatives come and go, one of the most powerful and often overlooked strategies is looking inward. What if the answers aren't out there, but already within our walls? By embedding these steps into an ongoing school improvement process, school administrators can ensure that successful teaching practices spread across classrooms. Let's outline how.

Step 1: Identify the "Who"

Start by gathering state testing and district benchmark results across multiple years. Look at the data with curiosity, analyzing it from multiple angles. Avoid averages, as they can be skewed by extreme scores. Instead, focus on percent proficiency and student growth over time.

Consider these key questions:

- Are there teachers whose students consistently outperform expectations?
- Do these results hold steady over the past two or three years?
- Are similar patterns evident when cross-referencing state assessments with district benchmark data?
- What trends emerge across grade levels or subject areas?

You might find that there is a second-grade teacher who gets outstanding assessment results year after year, even when the same group of students scored significantly lower the previous year in an earlier grade. Or there may be a social studies teacher whose students excel at writing claim-evidence-reasoning responses, sometimes surpassing the writing they produce in ELA classes. Both of these are causes for further exploration. Once you've identified who is getting exceptional results, the next step is to uncover how they're doing it so that others can learn, adapt, and benefit.

Step 2: Analyze the "What"

Now that the standout teachers are identified, the next step is to understand what they are doing differently. Gather a team of administrators, instructional coaches, and teacher leaders to observe their classrooms, looking for key instructional practices that contribute to student achievement.

These questions can guide the observations:

- How does the teacher foster student engagement and motivation?
- What strategies are used to maximize instructional time?
- How are curriculum materials utilized in ways that enhance learning?
- What research-based instructional strategies are evident?
- What does the classroom environment communicate about student learning?

As a team, determine the best method for gathering as much information as possible through these observations. It may be best to visit the classroom in pairs, being sure to capture all parts of the day in your observations. Having two perspectives is valuable because different people notice different things. Be transparent with the teacher, letting them know that they have been identified as having outstanding success and the purpose of the observations is to begin to determine the causes of success.

Going back to our examples, as you analyze classroom practices, you might notice that the second-grade teacher consistently uses quick, formative checks for understanding every ten minutes, adjusting instruction in real time based on student responses. Or you may observe that the social studies teacher uses visual sentence stems and structured peer feedback routines to support students in crafting strong evidence-based writing. These specific, replicable practices begin to reveal the "what" behind the success.

It is important to look for the throughlines, not just what the teacher is doing, but how those moves impact student learning. The goal isn't to celebrate isolated talent; it's to uncover strategies that can be named, shared, and adapted by others. These observations set the stage for our next step.

Step 3: Discover the "How"

After observations, engage in deeper conversations with the teacher to uncover the details behind their success. These discussions often reveal subtle yet impactful strategies that aren't immediately visible. These can be team-based or one-on-one conversations.

Guiding questions to ask:

- What do you believe are the keys to your students' success?
- How do you cultivate student motivation and investment in their learning?
- What strategies do you use to increase student cognitive engagement?
- How do you use instructional materials to support learning?
- Walk us through a lesson from beginning to end—what intentional choices do you make?

Teachers are often surprised by the depth of these discussions, realizing that what seems like second nature to them can be transformative when shared with colleagues. Across these conversations, four consistent themes emerge: teacher clarity, cognitive engagement, relational teaching, and supportive structure.

CAUSES OF STUDENT SUCCESS	
TEACHER CLARITY	**RELATIONAL TEACHING**
Teachers and students have clarity with: • the rigor of grade level expectations • the most important standards • effective instructional strategies • what success looks like • students' strengths and areas for growth.	Teachers express genuine belief in student potential. They create an environment where students feel valued and want to succeed in their learning. Students support and motivate each other. Teacher enthusiasm about learning creates an exciting classroom environment where students are eager and curious.
COGNITIVE ENGAGEMENT	**SUPPORTIVE STRUCTURE**
Intentional planning for effective instruciton leads to student engagement that goes beyond on-task behavior. Students lean into deep levels of thinking and communication. Effective questioning leads to visible student thinking through various forms of expression that demonstrate understanding and reasoning.	Teachers establish and uphold clear, consistent expectations for behavior, fostering a positive, structured environment where students feel safe, respected, and ready to learn. Students understand what to expect from their teacher, their peers, and what is expected of them.

A conversation with the second-grade teacher might reveal that she starts every day with a five-minute preview of that day's learning goals using student-friendly language, followed by a class-generated checklist that keeps students focused and accountable. She may share that she spirals key concepts weekly, ensuring students revisit and master essential skills over time.

The social studies teacher might share that, before introducing writing tasks, he models how to annotate primary sources using color coding and sentence starters. He might describe how he integrates short, timed writing sprints to build student confidence and fluency.

These aren't flashy programs, they're intentional choices rooted in clarity, structure, and trust in students' capabilities.

This step helps make the invisible visible. It's where routines, language, mindset, and relationships come into focus. When we pause to ask not just what works, but how teachers create the conditions for success, we uncover practices that are both powerful and replicable. These insights set the stage for scaling success, ensuring the wisdom of one becomes the collective strength of many.

Step 4: Scale the Success

Identifying best practices is only the first step. The real challenge is spreading these practices across the school. The key is creating structured, sustainable ways for teachers to learn from one another.

Practical Strategies for Scaling Success:

1. **Peer Observations:** Arrange for teachers to visit standout classrooms using the same observation guide from step 2. Encourage them to reflect on strategies they can implement in their own classrooms.
2. **Collaborative Planning Sessions:** Provide opportunities for teachers to co-plan lessons with high-impact educators, learning their approach firsthand.
3. **Lunch and Learns:** Create informal spaces where teachers can share and discuss instructional strategies over lunch.
4. **Teacher-Led Professional Development:** Instead of traditional PD sessions, empower teachers to lead learning based on their expertise and success.
5. **Action Research:** Encourage teachers to experiment with new strategies in a supportive, low-risk environment and reflect on the outcomes.

Teachers who observed the standout teacher could notice how her use of daily checklists helped students stay focused and take ownership of their learning. After a few peer visits, several colleagues adopt the strategy, tweaking it to fit their own classroom routines. Within weeks, students in multiple grades are referring to their checklist as part of their daily learning language.

Meanwhile, in the high school scenario, the social studies teacher hosted a Lunch and Learn to share how he uses structured peer feedback to strengthen writing. Colleagues from other departments attended, and one ELA teacher remarks, "I've been struggling to get students to revise their work meaningfully. This is a game-changer." That teacher later co-led a professional learning session, helping others build similar feedback structures in their own classrooms.

By creating space for teachers to observe, reflect, and try new ideas, schools move beyond isolated excellence. The practices that once lived in one classroom begin to spread organically, adapted through collaboration and sustained by shared ownership. This is how individual success becomes school-wide impact.

Addressing Common Barriers

Many teachers hesitate to showcase their strengths, fearing they'll appear boastful. They also deeply respect their colleagues' skills, making them reluctant to position themselves as experts. School leaders can ease these concerns by shifting the focus to collaboration over competition and framing the process as a way to improve student success collectively.

Additionally, no single teacher's approach will work for everyone. The goal isn't to replicate styles but to identify the core principles that drive success and empower all teachers to integrate them in ways that align with their unique classrooms. This process harnesses the power of collective efficacy, which John Hattie's research identifies as one of the most significant factors influencing student achievement.[1] When teachers believe in their collective ability to impact student learning, outcomes improve school-wide. Every teacher thrives when the entire team grows together—but growth doesn't mean uniformity. Instead, it means leveraging individual strengths within a shared commitment to excellence.

A Continuous Learning Cycle

Scaling instructional excellence isn't a one-time initiative, rather, it's an ongoing process. By using the Unlocking Pockets of Excellence cycle alongside Action Research, teachers can try new practices without fear of failure, and schools can refine strategies, adapt to new challenges, and ensure that best practices reach every classroom.

When schools commit to this process, the results extend beyond test scores, fostering engaged students, motivated teachers, and a thriving learning community. By building a culture of shared learning and continuous improvement, schools can transform isolated excellence into a school-wide standard of success. Excellence doesn't need to be invented. It needs to be noticed, nurtured, and shared. The answers are within our walls; we just have to unlock them.

KEY QUESTIONS TO MOVE FROM TALK INTO ACTION

1. Where in your school or district have you already seen evidence of instructional success, and how are you currently learning from it?
2. What structures or mindsets might be limiting your ability to recognize, share, or replicate what's working?
3. How can you create a culture where teachers feel safe and celebrated when sharing effective practices with colleagues?

Section 4

From Data to Impact

This section is about results, but not just the numbers, rather the stories behind them. Whether you're a classroom teacher or a school leader, these next two chapters will help you move beyond collecting data to actually using it to reflect, adjust, and accelerate growth.

For teachers, this section offers practical tools to track progress in real time, make sense of both quantitative and qualitative data, and connect daily instructional decisions to student success. You'll learn how to determine if a strategy is working, how to document impact meaningfully, and how to turn data into stories that celebrate learning and inform next steps.

For leaders, these chapters provide a road map for fostering a culture where results are visible, shared, and actionable. You'll explore how to support teams in telling the story behind the data, how to amplify what's working across classrooms, and how to use evidence to drive sustainable improvement.

Together, these chapters highlight an essential truth: data alone doesn't drive change—what we do with it does. When we gather the right evidence, reflect with intention, and share our learning with purpose, we move from isolated improvement to collective impact. That's when Action Research becomes not just a strategy but a catalyst for progress.

CHAPTER 8

Results

The Story in the Data

> *Results are important, but the way they are achieved, the process, is equally important.*
>
> —ROBERT GREENE

The best storytellers have us hanging on their every word. They lead us through moments that resonate and draw us into the experience. With vivid detail and carefully chosen words, they help us visualize what's happening and ignite our curiosity about what's coming next. The suspense, the anticipation, the connection that has us leaning in, eager for more—it's not just the mark of a good story, but a good storyteller.

Sometimes those stories come from a book we can't put down, a TV series we binge late into the night, or a movie that moves us to tears (or to cheers). But sometimes, the most powerful stories live in a place we don't expect, student data. Wait . . . what? Student data? Yes! Believe it or not, student data can anchor some of the most compelling stories we'll ever tell. The power doesn't reside in the numbers alone, it rests with the storyteller and how they use those numbers to reveal a change, track growth, and determine what's making the greatest impact.

State assessment results? We know what you might be thinking. Just hearing those words can increase anxiety. We've all sat through that data story: the unveiling of last year's scores, comparisons to district averages, or state benchmarks. We nod, we note, we plan goals and action steps that may or may not be reflective of what will actually happen in our classrooms. And by the time we see the next set of data, the story it's telling is old news, detached from the practices, challenges, and moments that shaped it. We are instead left guessing. We look for patterns, we make inferences, but we're reading the last page of a novel without knowing the characters or how they got there.

Let's write a different kind of story. A story that is grounded in results that are relevant, recent, and reflective of the work happening right now. This kind of story guides learning instead of just providing a reflection on it. It gives teachers immediate feedback on what's working and where to adjust. It sharpens instructional decision-making and makes learning outcomes visible. Most importantly, it transforms data into evidence of growth with clear indicators that our efforts are making a difference. You can hear it in the voices of teachers sharing what happened after piloting a fresh idea. You can see it in students' confidence as they realize they're improving. These are the stories that matter most. These are the stories that show results. These are the stories we should be telling.

One teacher team recently shared this story of results:

> We began by having students examine strong examples of commentary, using the success criteria in the writing rubric to identify what made them effective. Then, they applied this understanding by revising anonymous writing samples based on existing feedback.
>
> We then connected the feedback to the improved writing. As a result of this practice, 15% of students moved from "Standard Nearly Met" to "Standard Met" between their first and second brief writes. Even more exciting, 2%

reached the "Standard Exceeded" level. This showed us that short, focused practice with immediate feedback leads to better results.

Yes, the improvement in scores is exciting. But if we listen more closely, the students' voices reveal the impact of the change on results. Consider these examples:

- Before, when I would bomb a test or assignment, I would just quit. But the grade replacement policy gave me another chance and kept me from giving up midway through a unit, even when I didn't do well. There was always hope to bounce back.
- Catch-up days help with homework I couldn't do after school. Usually, when the school day is over, I'm burnt out. Having time in class to catch up and get help from my teacher made a big difference.

These reflections are the results. They are the qualitative data that deepen our understanding of quantitative progress. Together, they tell a complete story that captures effort, adaptation, and growth.

When transformative teacher teams engage in Action Research, all it takes is sitting in on one of their candid conversations to hear some of the most powerful stories about learning. Stories about what worked, what didn't, and the thoughtful steps taken along the way. Even better, step into their classrooms and talk with students about their work. These stories illuminate growth, celebrate success, and highlight the results that matter most to students and teachers alike.

Big Data, Small Data, Numbers, and Words

Which data best tells the story of your students' learning and helps shape the outcome you want for them? There's a difference between big data and small data. Big data, like summative tests, state assessments, benchmarks, and unit or semester exams, tells us how the chapter ends. In contrast, small data, such as common formative assessments (CFAs), captures learning while it's still happening.

CFAs allow grade-level or subject-area teams to check in on student understanding throughout instruction. They're quick, targeted, often ungraded, and provide timely feedback that can guide reteaching and immediate intervention. Unlike summative assessments, which offer a final evaluation and a grade, CFAs happen during learning and give students a chance to improve. That's why CFAs are essential for Action Research. They offer timely, actionable data that allows us to identify and address challenges in real time. Once those challenges emerge, we can narrow our focus and tackle one at a time.

Big data sets often span long periods and multiple standards, making it difficult to connect results to specific practices. As we mentioned before, it's like jumping to the end of a novel without understanding how the characters got there. Small data, like exit tickets, quick quizzes, and checks for understanding, reveal the twists and turns in the learning journey. Small data captures the impact of specific actions and strategies, making it easier to link causes (teacher practices) with effects (student outcomes). This helps determine next steps and signals when a course correction is needed.

Too often, data is reduced to numbers, percentages of proficiency, absence counts, graduation rates. These metrics are easy to collect, analyze, and compare, but they don't tell the whole story in the results. As Douglas Reeves notes, using data should feel more like a treasure hunt as we search for connection to our actions.[1] Yet our reliance on quantitative data overshadows the insights that come from qualitative sources. Qualitative data, on the other hand, uses descriptive words and open-ended responses to explain explain what happened, why, or how. It's more time-consuming to gather and analyze but adds essential context. It completes the narrative in ways numbers alone cannot.[2]

Consider these two examples that demonstrate combining quantitative and qualitative data to give more context to the results.

Example 1

In one science class, students struggled to write effective claim-evidence-reasoning (CER) responses. They had difficulty identifying claims and linking them to evidence. To address this, the team implemented sentence frames and clear rubrics. Students practiced evaluating samples and revising their own work. Initial assessments without sentence frames showed 70 percent meeting expectations. With frames, that jumped to 87 percent. On the final assessment, without frames again, 96 percent met expectations. Students reported that having the sentence frames helped to clarify what needed to be included for writing good claims and how to make connections between the evidence and the claims. They reported that they felt more comfortable and competent in their writing.

Example 2

In a high school class where all assignments had to be submitted digitally, 36 percent of graded work was missing. To address this, the teacher gave students the option to submit on paper. By the end of the semester, missing assignments dropped to 20 percent. Of the remaining missing assignments, just 15 percent were paper-based. The students reported that they were able to focus better when using the paper option. They also shared that sometimes they thought they had submitted digitally, had forgotten to do the final submissions, and had trouble with the digital submission process. Simplifying the submission process by offering a paper option eliminated some of the technical and remembering barriers.

In both cases, small, intentional changes led to measurable gains and meaningful feedback. Quantitative data showed the scale of impact. Qualitative insights explained why it worked. Together, they told a complete, actionable story—one that educators could use to guide what comes next.

Connecting Data to Results

Collecting data is only the beginning. To make meaningful instructional decisions, we must know how to interpret results and connect them back to the actions taken in the classroom. This process transforms data from static numbers into a dynamic narrative, a story that reveals student growth, instructional impact, and next steps. Action Research provides the framework for doing just that. The following steps can guide teacher teams through determining results in a way that is both practical and purposeful with real-time data.

Step 1: Select the Right Data for the Story You Want to Tell

- Include both quantitative data (e.g., CFAs, rubrics, assignment completion rates) and qualitative data (e.g., student reflections, teacher observations).
- Use small data collected in real time like exit tickets, quick quizzes, and student work samples to capture impact while learning is still in progress.

Step 2: Collect Data Before, During, and After the Change

- Establish a baseline (pre-data) using existing classroom assessments and information.
- Monitor student progress with regular check-ins and short assessments during the implementation.
- Capture post-data to compare and determine growth or change.

Step 3: Document Student and Teacher Voice

- Use surveys, written reflections, or interviews to gather students' feedback on their learning experience.

- As the teacher, reflect on what worked, what surprised you, and what could be improved.

Step 4: Analyze Results to Link Practice and Impact

- Look for patterns in the quantitative results (e.g., growth in scores, reduction in missing work).
- Use qualitative insights to interpret the "why" behind the changes.
- Make comparisons across data points to determine if the strategy led to measurable, meaningful growth.

Step 5: Use the Result to Write the Story of Learning

- Synthesize findings into a clear, brief narrative: what was tried, what changed, and what it means.
- Include both student outcomes and teacher reflections to bring the story to life.
- Share your story with colleagues to fuel further innovation and reflection.

Step 6: Decide What Comes Next

- Based on results, choose to:
    - refine and expand the strategy,
    - try a new approach to address another challenge, or
    - continue collecting data for longer-term impact.

When we take the time to thoughtfully gather, examine, and reflect on results, we begin to see that data shows us where learning is happening and where more support is needed. These steps help us link strategies to outcomes, making the story of student learning both visible and actionable. Most importantly, they reinforce that small, intentional changes, when paired with thoughtful data collection, can lead to significant results. This is how Action Research becomes more than a project. It becomes a way of thinking, learning, and improving together.

KEY QUESTIONS TO MOVE FROM TALK INTO ACTION

1. What story does your student data tell, and how clearly does it connect to the actions you've taken in your classroom?
2. How will you balance both quantitative and qualitative data to fully capture the impact of your teaching?
3. How will you add student voice to your story of results?

CHAPTER 9

Sharing Impact

Telling the Right Story

> *The results of our work must not only be measured but also made visible—because what gets shared, gets improved.*
>
> —MICHAEL FULLAN

Picture this: a gymnasium is buzzing not with a scoreboard buzzer but with energy. Over two hundred educators stand proudly beside trifold boards that showcase their learning. Each display tells a story: a student learning challenge identified, a strategy implemented, results with both data and reflections, all captured with intention. Teachers don't just talk about their work; they own it. They share what worked and what didn't. They reflect on their students' growth. They quote students, highlight "aha" moments, and celebrate shifts in learning. The superintendent walks through the aisles, moved by the energy. This isn't a motivational keynote. This is authentic, community-driven professional learning.

Now contrast that with a more typical scene: a group of teachers in a conference room listening to a presenter. Best case, they leave with a few ideas to try. Worst case, they're disengaged, quietly wondering how else they could have used their time. We've led both types of experiences. And we know which one leads to real change. That's the difference made by Action Research.

The first scenario described above is a creative and effective way to share Action Research findings through a Teacher Science Fair or Exhibition of Learning. Modeled after student science fairs, this event provides us with an opportunity to present our classroom investigations, evidence, and results to peers, administrators, and community members.

Each teacher or team sets up a display that outlines:

- the student challenge they addressed,
- the strategy or intervention they implemented,
- the quantitative and qualitative results they collected, and reflections and next steps.

The format can include trifold boards, digital presentations, or interactive visuals. Visitors circulate, ask questions, and engage in dialogue about what was learned and how it can be applied in other contexts. This celebration of learning not only elevates teacher voice and agency but fosters a culture of shared learning and innovation.

While the Learning Exhibition is one way to put our results on display, there are other ways in which results can be shared. Whatever the chosen format, in districts where this approach has been implemented, teachers report feeling more confident, validated, and motivated to continue using Action Research as a tool for continuous improvement.

So many incredible learning moments happen each day in our classrooms. One of the biggest missed opportunities is not sharing those moments with others who could learn from them. These shared experiences can be some of the most powerful forms of professional learning. When teachers talk about the specific actions they took to meet learning needs, everyone benefits. Not only do we amplify what works, but we also build a culture of transparency and collaboration, where success is not isolated but scaled across classrooms and schools.

As we focus on what's happening in our own classrooms, we often discover that the challenges we face aren't unique. The same struggles and solutions exist in classrooms just down the hall. These stories, when shared, build collective wisdom. They weave a thread from challenge to action to results, linking teacher intentions to real student outcomes. And in doing so, they highlight what matters most: practices that make a difference.

Think of the challenge as the opening scene, the practices as the plot, and the results as the resolution. Through this lens, the data becomes a narrative. It's not just about scores or statistics but also understanding the journey of learning. And when the story is clear, the results become a call to action, a road map for others to follow, or a springboard for further inquiry.

Good storytellers craft vivid images. Action researchers must do the same. Whether through trifold boards, slide decks, or one-pagers, creating visuals and a story allows peers to replicate the same steps to improvement in their own classrooms. What's important is making the learning visible, not just sharing *what* changed, but *how* it changed and *why* it mattered. With clear visuals and intentional storytelling, results become more than data points. They become catalysts for shared growth.

Reflecting with Intention

Through the many Learning Exhibitions we've facilitated, several key questions have emerged that help teams reflect and prepare to share.

- What was your challenge?
- What changes or practices did you implement?
- What results have you seen (quantitative and qualitative)?
- What barriers did you encounter?
- What was the student response?
- What surprised you?

- What would you do differently?

When teachers share their challenge/practice/results with each other, powerful learning occurs. Responses to these questions help fill in the details to paint the picture of success.

Challenge
Teachers noticed that there were high rates of Ds and Fs due to missing work in biology classes.
Practice
Because some students struggle with focus and sometimes need additional assistance, the decision was made to assign students to the school's lunchtime academic support. This was provided so students can work on missing assignments during their lunch period. This happened daily to provide immediate intervention to get missing work completed. Individual teachers monitored turn-in and completion rates and followed up when students failed to attend.
Results
Teachers saw positive results from assigning lunchtime academic support to students with three or more missing assignments. There was a reduction from fifty-seven missing assignments to twenty-seven missing assignments during the grading period (almost a 50 percent reduction). This reduction is attributed to students having extra time and support to finish assignments, and many were more motivated to complete their work on time to avoid missing social time with their friends. Implementation started later during the year but showed good results. This strategy will start at the beginning of next school year so students don't fall so far behind. After much grumbling, students appreciated the allocated time and the accountability to get their work done.

Now think about how this structured process might be used to share results from classroom practices in your school.

Activity: The Story Behind the Results

Purpose: Help teams reflect on a recent strategy or intervention, connect it to student outcomes, and communicate results in a clear, narrative format.

Materials: Chart paper, sticky notes, or digital templates

Time: 30–45 minutes

Step 1: Set the Stage
Prompt: "Every data point has a story. Let's uncover the story your classroom data is trying to tell."

Step 2: Complete the Story Frame
Use these sentence frames to guide reflection:

- "We noticed that . . ." (Challenge)
- "So we decided to . . ." (Action)
- "We collected data by . . ." (Evidence)
- "What surprised us was . . ." (Surprise)
- "One student said . . ." or "We saw students . . ." (Student Voice)
- "As a result, we saw . . ." (Results)
- "Now, we're planning to . . ." (Next Step)

Step 3: Share Out
Teams present their story aloud or on a gallery wall.

- Audience members share back what resonated or ask follow-up questions.

Knowing Your Impact

"Know thy impact."[1] John Hattie's words resonate with educators who reflect deeply on their practice. But to truly know our impact, we must go beyond scores and collect the right evidence. Big data or small data. Quantitative or qualitative. Action Research helps teachers decide which data best captures their success and supports growth.

When we treat results as more than numbers and connect them to our stories, our students, and our practice, we transform data from something done to us into something driven by us. Action Research doesn't just illuminate what worked, it reveals why, how, and what it means next. And when we share these stories with purpose, we don't just improve practice. We inspire it.

KEY QUESTIONS TO MOVE FROM TALK INTO ACTION

1. What story is your classroom and school data trying to tell?
2. How will you make your results visible and actionable?
3. Who needs to hear your story of student growth, and how will you share it in a way that inspires learning and action?

Section 5

Building Collective Efficacy Through Action Research

This section is about what happens when Action Research moves beyond the individual and becomes part of a shared culture, when leaders, teams, and students all engage in inquiry, reflection, and growth together.

For school leaders, these chapters offer a clear framework for leading with curiosity, clarity, and courage. You'll discover how to model the risk-taking and reflective learning you want to see in your staff, how to turn data into direction, and how to build a culture where improvement is driven by shared purpose, not compliance. You'll find practical examples, coaching strategies, and guiding questions to help you lead professional learning that truly sticks.

For teachers, this section shows how Action Research can transform not just individual practice, but the entire experience of collaboration and student learning. You'll see how teams move from surface-level exchange to meaningful, student-centered inquiry. And then we'll explore how students themselves can become researchers of their own learning.

Together, these chapters illuminate a powerful truth: when leaders go first, when teams lean in, and when students take ownership, Action Research becomes a powerful path forward for all of us. It turns goals from distant aspirations into shared accomplishments that are grounded in evidence, fueled by collaboration, and sustained by a culture of continuous learning.

CHAPTER 10

Leading Through Action Research

> *A leader is one who knows the way,*
> *goes the way and shows the way.*
>
> —JOHN C. MAXWELL

"Take it for what it's worth." This is not the phrase you want to hear as you're introduced to a group of teachers you will be working with for the day. But it is exactly the phrase one principal said to the crowd as he turned a learning session over to Emily. It was one of her first outings as an instruction and leadership coach, and she had been contracted to support these particular teachers with practical classroom management strategies.

When the principal turned and walked out of the room, it felt like the day may have been ruined before it even began. After an awkward silence, Emily smiled and with enthusiasm said, "And I know it is going to be worth a lot!" At the end of their learning time together, as they were sharing out what they would implement immediately and how they would support one another with common strategies, one teacher sighed and muttered, "It sure would have been nice if our principal had heard all of this too." Boy, do we agree!

While this day ended up being valuable to the teachers, their principal's participation in the learning would have made it even more so.

They would have known he was in this with them, had a shared understanding of the work ahead, and was committed to supporting their implementation steps. His flippant comment as he turned the microphone over to Emily that morning spoke volumes to the teachers. He said, "Take it for what it's worth," but the teachers heard:

- You don't need to learn and change. You just need to get through the PD session today. So, take it for what it's worth.
- I am not sure you are capable of changing, so take it for what it's worth.
- PD is super boring to me, and it probably is to you, so take it for what it's worth.

Now, this may not have been the principal's intention, but vague, offhand comments like his can be interpreted in ways that undermine the very learning we hope to support. Fortunately, Emily had the opportunity to provide the principal with coaching and feedback after the PD session.

Using an Action Research approach, she asked: "How might principal participation in professional learning impact teacher engagement and implementation?" She reviewed teacher reflections and noted the recurring theme of absent leadership. She also observed how the room's energy shifted when the principal left, compared to the strong collaboration that developed by the end.

Emily invited the principal to debrief. Rather than dwell on the comment, she shared the teachers' feedback and asked, "What might have changed if you had stayed to experience the learning alongside your teachers?"

The principal was initially defensive, listing tasks that had pulled him away. Emily gently pressed on: "Let's talk about the comment you made when introducing me. What message do you think it sent when you said, 'Take it for what it's worth'?"

With a slight drop of his head, he paused. "Honestly," he said, "I didn't think about how it might land. But now I see it may have set the wrong tone from the start."

And just like that, the real learning began, not only for the teachers, but for the leader too. Together, they developed a plan for future sessions where the principal would not only attend but actively participate and model implementation. Emily offered to provide coaching before and after each session to help the principal prepare and reflect.

When leaders hear the same message as teachers, engage in the conversations teachers have with each other, ask questions to understand and clarify goals and expectations, and explore the challenges and benefits of implementation, meaningful change takes root. Teachers see firsthand the leader's willingness to invest in their own growth and their commitment to supporting the efforts of the teachers.[1] This is the very opposite of the "do as I say and not as I do" model employed by many leaders, who focus more on getting things done than on leading for results. Maxwell reminds us, "Followers may doubt what their leaders say, but they usually believe what they do."[2]

Leaders Who Pull Up a Chair

Now, contrast that moment with another school, where the leadership team is fully engaged in the same Action Research process as teachers. At one table, the principal, assistant principals, and instructional coaches are poring over walkthrough data, analyzing how consistently Tier 1 practices are being implemented and whether those practices are impacting student engagement and understanding.

They examine trends, identify gaps, and discuss what's working and what needs refining. Their focus is clear: find a few high-impact practices, ensure consistency, and support staff with the tools and feedback they need to succeed.

Teachers look across the room and see their leaders immersed in the same work, asking hard questions, grappling with evidence, and planning actionable next steps. This model of participatory leadership sends a powerful message: we're in this together.

And that message changes everything.

Lead with Learning

In *Radical Candor*, Kim Scott writes,

> When you become the boss, you are under the microscope. People do listen to you in an intense way you never experienced before you became a manager. They attribute meaning—sometimes accurately, sometimes not—to what you say, to the clothes you wear, to the car you drive. In some ways, becoming a boss is like getting arrested. Everything you say or do can and will be used against you.[3]

As educational leaders, whether we like it or not, our people are constantly watching us. They examine and scrutinize our words and our actions. They seek validation by determining if what we say matches what we do. If we want teachers to invest in their own learning and to be willing to consider new practices, we have to do so ourselves and take on the role of lead learner.

"You go first!" How many times over the course of your childhood did you hear that challenge dropped when one of your friends had the bright idea to do something daring? On the playground, in the neighborhood, in our own backyards, or even in places your parents specifically instructed you not to go? And in most cases, someone would step up. Those of us who were reluctant were then able to muster up courage we didn't realize we had because someone else forged the path.

This experience is not unique to childhood. It also anchors much of what happens with teachers when they encounter new initiatives and classroom practices. But what if, instead of looking around to see which of their teacher colleagues was brave enough to go first, their leader simply stepped out in front first?

In *What Makes a Great Principal*, Emily shares the story of a principal who did exactly that.[4] This particular principal came back from a conference with the idea to have teachers utilize microteaching for professional reflection and growth. When he introduced this idea to his leadership team, you guessed it, one of them said, "You should go first!" After some hemming and hawing, he accepted the challenge and became the model.

Despite his discomfort, he developed and recorded a reading lesson he delivered to a third-grade class. By the way, he had been a middle school math teacher before moving into an administrative role and had never taught a reading lesson. He shared his video with the staff as he asked them to join in this learning journey. They debriefed about what he did to plan for and deliver his lesson, and they unpacked the feelings of anxiousness, excitement, and success he felt throughout the process. He later shared that teachers had expressed to him that they were only willing to try microteaching themselves because he had done it first.

There is a tendency of leaders to downplay the significance of their participation alongside teachers, and this is a huge misstep that can undermine an initiative from the outset. When school leaders invest in their own learning and walk the path with teachers as they learn, everyone benefits. Leaders understand what they are asking of teachers, teachers know leaders are invested and supportive, and students reap the rewards through better classroom experiences. For the principal above, "the collective learning on his staff was transformed, all because he was willing to go first."[5] He embraced that, as the leader, it was up to him to forge the path and modeled the way.

Leaning into Challenge

As humans, we tend to stick with what's comfortable. It's just how we're wired. That pull toward the familiar can keep us from stepping into the unknown even when we know that's where real change happens. How many times have we hesitated to do what we know is right because we feared overwhelming others? How many times have we taken the path of least resistance and settled for "good enough"?

We can all accept that change is hard. Leadership is hard. But doing what's best for students? That should never feel out of reach. This is where we, as leaders, have to make a choice: we can pull back, or we can push through. We can let discomfort hold us back, or we can lean into the challenge and lead forward.

A great place to start is with data and the voices of our school community. The information we need to identify pressing issues is almost always right in front of us. When leaders take time to gather input and prioritize a single, school-wide challenge, whether it's chronic absenteeism, improving Tier 1 instruction, or managing student cell phone use, they set the stage for meaningful, focused action. That clarity becomes the foundation for leadership-driven Action Research.

At one school, leaders dug into walkthrough data and noticed an imbalance in classroom discourse. Teacher talk dominated instructional time, leaving little room for students to engage in meaningful academic conversation. Knowing that student talk leads to deeper thinking, they set a clear expectation: every teacher would incorporate structured discussion protocols into instruction. Support followed. During staff meetings and collaborative team time, teachers were introduced to new strategies. Instructional coaches provided models and opportunities for practice. Then came the follow-up classroom visits.

But the next round of walkthroughs showed little change.

Instead of throwing up their hands or placing blame, the leaders took a step back. At the next staff meeting, they shared what they had seen and clarified their expectations: every fifteen minutes, students should be engaged in purposeful academic talk, whether as a check for understanding, peer feedback, or a quick reflection. They even aligned their data collection method with that expectation: if observers stayed in a classroom for at least fifteen minutes, they should see a discussion protocol in action.

Sure enough, during the next round of observations, the shift was clear. Student talk had increased significantly. Teachers were using the protocols consistently, and the classroom energy had changed. What made the difference? It wasn't just the expectation, it was the clarity, the support, and the shared ownership of the work.

Had those leaders stopped after the second round of walkthroughs, they would've missed the breakthrough. Instead, they leaned in. They reflected. They adjusted. Their willingness to stay in it with teachers changed practices and culture.

Real is not standing on the sidelines. It's jumping in, especially when things are messy and the path forward isn't perfectly mapped out. When leaders engage in Action Research alongside their teachers, they show them that they're all in it together.

KEYS TO ACTION RESEARCH FOR LEADERS:

1. Model the "try-in" method and risk-taking you want to see from teachers.
2. Learn shoulder-to-shoulder with staff to communicate the importance of continuous learning. As a side benefit, you will also develop stronger, more trusting relationships.
3. Let data guide your leadership, not just your decisions. Use qualitative and quantitative data to identify real challenges, test solutions, and evaluate impact—with full transparency.
4. Stay in the learning loop. Don't stop after the first cycle. Keep observing, reflecting, adjusting, and supporting implementation until meaningful change takes hold.
5. Lead with visibility and vulnerability. Be present, ask questions, admit what you're learning. This builds credibility and fosters collective ownership.

6. Prioritize clarity over compliance. When expectations are clear, aligned to purpose, and reinforced through coaching, teachers feel supported rather than micromanaged.
7. Go first. Then walk with. Whether it's modeling a lesson, trying a new protocol, or reflecting publicly on your learning, you lead best by doing.

In this kind of environment, Action Research becomes a way of being. It becomes an integral part of the culture. And when leaders lead with courage, clarity, and connection, they build communities where everyone believes in what's possible and is willing to do the work to get there.

That's the kind of leadership that lasts. That's the kind that changes lives.

KEY QUESTIONS TO MOVE FROM TALK INTO ACTION:

1. Every educator is a leader. In what ways do your actions as a leader model the type of learning and risk-taking outlined in this chapter?
2. How can you more actively engage in the learning process alongside teachers or colleagues to build trust and collective efficacy?
3. What challenge in your school could become the focus of leadership-driven Action Research, and how can you involve others in addressing it?

CHAPTER 11

Action Research for High-Performing Teams

> *The strength of the team is each individual member.*
> *The strength of each member is the team.*
>
> —PHIL JACKSON

Every educator has sat through a meeting that felt like a waste of time. Think back to the last one you attended. Now estimate the hourly wages of everyone in the room. Add them together and consider what that meeting cost, not just in dollars, but in time, energy, and lost momentum. It's astonishing, isn't it? Meetings are too expensive to waste. But what if they became the most powerful lever for student success in the school?

Too often, teacher teams operate at a transactional level—they share materials or logistics but stop short of the kind of deep collaboration that truly impacts student learning. Action Research offers a way forward. It's a practical framework for moving beyond surface-level exchanges toward meaningful, transformative teamwork, where inquiry, evidence, and shared responsibility lead to real results.

This chapter is about helping teacher teams move from good intentions to transformative work that drives real results for students. We'll explore what makes some teams thrive, why others get stuck, and how schools can create the systems and relationships that fuel collective efficacy.

And it all starts with a simple but surprisingly revealing question we recently heard from a teacher: "Wait, we have to be trained on how to have a team meeting?"

It's a fair question with a not-so-simple answer. Like many things in education, it depends. If your goal is to have a transactional team where teachers share lesson ideas, discuss pacing, make copies, and maybe grab each other coffee, you probably don't need training. Most educators work together in congenial, cooperative ways. But our students need more. They need us to move beyond transactional relationships.

This isn't a one-or-the-other scenario. Transformative teams still value positive social interactions and strong relationships, but they don't stop there. They dig deeper. They engage in meaningful dialogue, wrestle with practice, and hold each other accountable to ambitious goals. Coming together for a common purpose in our schools is so powerful and so needed. We're not aiming for students to have one great year or one great teacher. We want every student to experience great teaching and deep learning every year of their academic career. And that requires more than congeniality and good intentions; it requires transformative teams.

Coaching and support are crucial for teacher teams striving toward transformation. But it's important to acknowledge that most professional relationships in schools are still transactional, which limits their impact. Transactional relationships often stop at politely exchanging information. Transformational relationships go further, and they require vulnerability, candor, and a shared commitment to student success.

Here's the good news: our teams already have the power to make that shift. Moving teams from transactional to transformative opens the door to collective efficacy. Decades of research, from John Hattie's meta-analyses to Rachel Eells's dissertation, highlight that when teacher teams believe in their collective power and work toward a shared goal, student achievement rises.[1] But belief isn't enough; it must be paired with systems that support the work.

So, how do transactional teams interact, and how is that different from how transformative teams interact? The table below helps us analyze the difference in actions between transactional teams and transformative teams so we can understand how to make the shift and identify our team's strengths and areas for growth.

Shifting Teams from TRANSACTIONAL to TRANSFORMATIVE

Transactional Teams	Transformative Teams
• Focus on tasks	• Focus on growth
• Relationships are surface-level and are centered on day-to-day	• Relationships centered on trust, risk-taking, and reciprocal vulnerability
• Efficiency-driven	• Impact-driven
• Plan together, make copies for each other, share resources	• Have shared goals that center on results
• May create cliques and marginalize some members	• Value all team members equally
• Problem-solve things like tech issues, customer complaints, etc.	• Share data to learn from each other and customers
• Buy each other coffee	• Understand that they can make a difference through ongoing development and teamwork.
• Provide emotional support	• Also buy each other coffee

If you are like us, you appreciate an easy-to-follow formula. Tapping into the transformative power of collective efficacy is not simple, but here are steps your school team or teacher teams (or leadership teams, or any teams) can take to begin to bridge the gap between transactional and transformative teaming.

1. **Clarify Purpose and Set a Collaboration Goal:** Start by developing a shared understanding of what effective collaboration looks like and why it matters. Use the "Shifting Teams" chart or a team self-assessment to reflect on your current strengths and challenges. Then, choose one specific goal to strengthen your collaboration and move toward transformational practice.

   One team we supported enjoyed working together. They planned lessons, shared resources, and brought each other Starbucks every Friday. But when they used the "Shifting Teams" chart, they realized their collaboration rarely went deeper than surface-level. They agreed on a goal to create space for deeper conversations about student learning, starting by dedicating part of each meeting to reviewing data and co-planning support strategies. By focusing on a shared purpose and one clear goal, they began to shift how they worked together, and the results followed.

2. **Establish Supportive Systems:** Put structures in place that make collaboration purposeful, efficient, and sustainable. This includes using consistent agendas, defining clear roles (like facilitator, timekeeper, and notetaker), agreeing on shared norms, and ending each meeting with an action plan.

   A high school ELA team realized their meetings often felt disorganized and reactive. By adopting a simple agenda template aligned to their instructional goals, rotating roles, and ending each meeting by setting the agenda for the next, they increased both productivity and accountability without adding more meetings to their calendars.

3. **Leverage Individual Strengths:** Get to know each team member's strengths, interests, and preferred ways of contributing. Use this insight to distribute leadership, recognize effort, and build a culture where everyone feels seen and valued.

At one elementary school, a team started using a simple "team inventory" to capture each person's areas of expertise and what kind of recognition made them feel appreciated. One teacher loved organizing data, while another was a creative lesson designer. The team intentionally leaned into these strengths and created space for each person to shine, transforming the group dynamic from cooperative to collaborative.

4. **Set and Monitor Student-Centric Goals:** Establish clear, measurable goals that prioritize student learning, and develop a system for tracking progress over time. Revisit the data regularly to assess impact and make adjustments.

   For example, one middle school math team noticed that while their students performed well on simple computations, they struggled with multi-step problems and real-world applications. They decided to make math discourse their initial focus, setting a goal to incorporate structured problem-solving discussions into lessons at least three times per week. Starting with one shared goal helped them build momentum and confidence for deeper work ahead.

Once a team has defined a shared purpose, set clear goals, and established supportive systems, they're ready for deeper work. Moving from surface-level collaboration to truly transformational learning takes trust and reciprocal vulnerability. Teams must be willing to name challenges honestly, even when one person's challenge is another's strength. That kind of transparency allows for meaningful learning rooted in real experience. Action Research provides a powerful framework for that kind of growth. It gives teacher teams a structured, student-centered process to identify challenges, test strategies, analyze results, and adapt based on what they learn together.

Who Makes Up a Teacher Team?

It depends.

The makeup of a teacher team should reflect the goal they're trying to achieve. The collective intelligence of the group is what accelerates progress, but only when it's composed of the right people working on the right challenge. In *Collective Intelligence*, Woolley, Aggarwal, and Malone describe two common ways teams are set up to fail: they're given tasks that aren't well suited for group work, or they're assigned vague, unclear goals.[2]

To avoid these pitfalls and harness the power of collective efficacy, every team needs three essential elements:

- **Valued Membership:** Team members must be equally respected and engaged in pursuit of the shared goal.
- **Clear Goals:** Each team must know exactly what it's working toward. If there are multiple goals, consider tackling them one at a time or breaking into subteams.
- **Aligned Purpose:** Teams should ask, "Is this goal best accomplished together rather than through individual work?" If the answer is yes, you're ready to collaborate.

Do team members have to teach the same grade level? The same subject? Do they all need to be teachers? Do they have to stay the same all year long? No, no, no, and no.

Teams can be flexible and responsive. They may be homogeneous or heterogeneous, consistent or rotating. What matters most is that the composition aligns with the goal. That's why we appreciate the term used by Dr. Douglas Reeves and the team at Creative Leadership Solutions, "collaborative learning teams" (CLTs). This term captures both the collaborative process and the shared commitment to learning for students and educators.

Whatever the composition, CLTs function best when there are consistent expectations for how they'll work together. Something as simple as sitting in a circle so that no one has their back to someone else can subtly and powerfully communicate that every voice is valued. That visual cue, paired with shared norms and intentional routines, lays the foundation for the kind of honest, purpose-driven collaboration needed for successful Action Research.

Implementing Action Research as a Team

One of the greatest strengths of Action Research is its flexibility. It can be used by an individual teacher, a small group, or even scaled across an entire school or district. But when teams engage in Action Research together, the impact multiplies. That's because it combines the power of structured inquiry with the force of collective efficacy. The steps below can serve as a guide for teams looking to transform and expand their impact on student learning.

1. **Identify a shared challenge:** This is the fun part, the opportunity to get curious with data. What common challenges are you noticing when you look at data in the form of student work, assessment results, behavior trends, or anecdotal evidence? Identify a challenge that has meaning for everyone around the table.

    Example: A high school science team noticed that in many of their classrooms, only a handful of students consistently participated in academic discussions. The majority remained passive, even when prompted. Their shared challenge: low student participation in whole-class and small-group discussions.

2. **Ask team-wide inquiry questions:** This is a great place to use the Collaborative Learning Team anchor questions.[3]
    - Standards: What do we want students to know and be able to do?
    - Assessment: How will students demonstrate their level of understanding?

- Instruction: What Tier 1 strategies will we use to ensure students reach proficiency?
- Differentiation: What strategies will we use to reteach *and* extend learning based on the data?

  Example: The high school science team crafted the question "What impact does the consistent use of structured discussion protocols have on student participation in academic conversations during science instruction?"

3. **Design a shared strategy:** Select one research-informed strategy to implement as a team. This could be a high-impact practice already used successfully in your school or one identified through a trusted research source. Agree on key implementation details, including how often the strategy will be used, the duration of the trial period, and clear expectations for consistency across classrooms.

   Example: The science team selected two simple, research-based discussion protocols (such as Think-Pair-Share) and committed to using one of them at least three times per week in every classroom. They aligned on when and how the protocols would be used, ensuring consistency.

4. **Collect evidence together:** Decide what evidence you'll gather and how. Keep it manageable and meaningful. Options include student work samples, rubrics, surveys, exit slips, or observation notes.

   Example: Each science teacher chose a group of three focus students (including one frequent participant, one occasional participant, and one reluctant speaker). They used a simple observation tool to record participation levels during discussions and collected short student reflections each week.

5. **Analyze and reflect as a team:** Come back together regularly to look at the evidence. What's improving? What's not? What trends do you notice? Reflection is the engine of Action

Research because it helps teams make sense of the work and deepen their understanding of what's working and why.

Example: After three weeks, the science team met to review participation data and student feedback. They found that students who previously were hesitant to speak were more likely to contribute when they had time to think first and knew the discussion structure in advance. One teacher noticed that using sentence stems helped scaffold participation for English learners, and this strategy began spreading across the team.

6. **Adjust and repeat:** Based on your reflection, adjust the strategy or move into a second cycle. The beauty of Action Research is that it's continuous. Each cycle builds on the last, giving you a chance to refine your approach and improve student outcomes along the way.

    Example: The science team agreed to continue using the protocols but added an additional layer: they would co-create discussion norms with students and incorporate peer-led conversations. In the next cycle, they planned to study the impact of student facilitation on both participation and depth of discussion.

When we step back and consider what our teams are capable of, not just as individuals, but as a collective, it's hard not to feel a sense of awe. The shift from transactional to transformative collaboration does not make our work harder; it actually makes it easier because we are working together with intention, purpose, and trust. We are creating the kind of clarity and shared ownership where every voice matters and every action moves us closer to what students deserve.

When we build systems that support meaningful collaboration and invest in relationships that fuel real growth, powerful things happen. And that power? It doesn't come from a new program or a top-down mandate. It comes from your colleagues, your teams, your community.

So let's stop waiting for change to come from somewhere else. Let's roll up our sleeves, pull our chairs into a circle, and do the work that transforms not just our schools but each other.

KEY QUESTIONS TO MOVE FROM TALK INTO ACTION

1. Where is your team currently on the spectrum from transactional to transformative, and what is one step you can take to move forward?
2. What challenge could your team investigate through Action Research that would make a meaningful difference for your students?
3. How might greater clarity, shared purpose, and reciprocal trust change the way your team collaborates, and what impact could that have on student success?

CHAPTER 12

Empowering Student Learners Through Action Research

> *We learn by doing, if we reflect on what we are doing.*
>
> —JOHN DEWEY

Because we truly believe in the power of Action Research to transform learning at every level, we know it is essential to involve students in the process. Too often, school improvement efforts are done to students instead of with them. Students are positioned as passive recipients of interventions, strategies, and systems designed by adults. But what if we flipped that dynamic? What if students became active participants in their own learning, using the same Action Research framework that empowers teachers and teams?

Action Research engages students in reflective inquiry, which helps them move from compliance to curiosity, from confusion to ownership. In this chapter, we'll explore how teachers can guide students to become researchers of their own learning and how that shift deepens both academic and personal growth.

We've accomplished so much together in this book:

- We've explored what Action Research is and how it can strengthen our instructional practices.
- We've learned how to align strategies with the challenges that get in the way of student learning.
- We've gained clarity on how to measure the impact of the practices we implement.
- We've discovered the power of sharing our Action Research to grow through collaboration.
- We've examined how to move teams from transactional work to transformational shared purpose.
- And we've uncovered the steps to leveraging the success that is already within our schools and districts.

In this final chapter, we'll do something exciting: we'll look at how to bring Action Research into the classroom with students, helping them become reflective, empowered learners who take ownership of their growth. Because real improvement doesn't come from the top down or the outside in; it comes from learning together, reflecting together, and moving forward together.

Have you ever had this moment in your classroom? Students are working quietly, you're circulating the room, and a hand goes up. You walk over and ask, "What's your question?" The student shrugs and says, "I don't understand."

You follow up: "What don't you understand?"

And then comes the dreaded response: "All of it."

Now you know it'll take a series of questions to uncover where the confusion really begins. As you guide the student step by step, you're not just helping them learn, you're modeling how to think about their thinking.

A situation such as this is where Action Research can be such a gift. It gives students the tools to start identifying for themselves where they're getting stuck, and more importantly, it offers a process for how they might move forward. When we invite students into this process, we're not just helping them learn better, we're helping them become more aware, in control, and engaged in their own growth.

Action Research can be a powerful instructional tool when used with students, because it allows them to become more active participants in their own learning journey. They are able to identify where they are experiencing challenges and focus on areas they are interested in improving. Rather than passively receiving information, students can engage with their own questions or challenges, like figuring out how to improve their study habits, work better with classmates, or grasp a tricky concept.

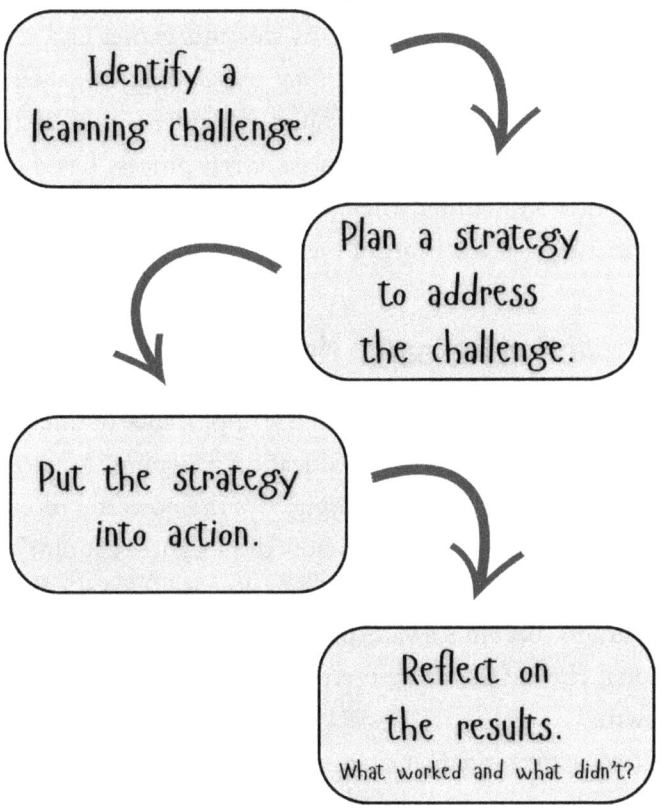

With gentle guidance from the teacher, students can walk through the same cycle of inquiry that has them identify a problem or challenge they are experiencing in their learning, plan a strategy, put it into action, and reflect on the results. Along the way, they build deeper content knowledge while strengthening essential skills like critical thinking, communication, and problem-solving.[1]

In the classroom, Action Research provides students the opportunity and process to analyze how they learn best. It helps them become better at diagnosing their own misunderstandings and learning challenges. It encourages them to reflect, set goals, and try new strategies to improve.

Imagine students investigating which study methods help them remember more before a quiz or how peer feedback makes their writing stronger. What if they were able to ask specific questions that zero in on the errors in their learning? As students gather and analyze data they collect about the strategies they use to improve their learning, they begin to see themselves not just as students, but as researchers of their own progress. The Action Research process has the power to create a classroom culture where curiosity, reflection, and continuous improvement are at the heart of everything we do.

Action Research Meets Metacognition

Most educators begin hearing about the importance of "metacognition" when they get into their college education programs. Metacognition is simply thinking about your thinking.[2] It's the powerful moment when a student pauses and says, "Wait, how did I figure that out?" or "What could I try differently next time?" It's the aha moment that happens when learners become aware of how they learn and start making intentional choices about their strategies, their focus, and their learning growth.

When we promote metacognition in the classroom, we go beyond only teaching content by helping students develop the skill of reflection.

We help students see that learning is not just about getting the correct answer, but it's also about being curious and determining the thinking needed to get to that answer. The learning process becomes about trusting that every mistake is just another step on the way to better understanding.

Action Research gives structure to metacognition. It turns "thinking about your thinking" into a repeatable cycle: identify a challenge, try a strategy, reflect on what works, and adapt. In doing so, it transforms abstract reflection into concrete, actionable learning. Through Action Research, we can nurture metacognition by helping students think deeply about *how* they learn, not just *what* they learn.

In one school, a team of math teachers wanted to deepen students' understanding and encourage more perseverance when tackling tough problems. Together, they came up with a small shift that made a big difference. Instead of writing scores on students' tests, they simply marked each answer as correct or incorrect. That was it—no percentages, no grades, just feedback.

When students got their tests back, they were asked to do three tasks. First, they reworked the problems they had missed, either independently or with the support of a peer. Next, they identified the specific mistake they had made and wrote a short explanation of how they corrected it. Finally, they reflected on what they would remember the next time they faced a similar problem.

Rather than just focusing on getting the right answer, this approach was about helping students slow down, notice their thinking, and grow from it. Reflection became the real learning. It wasn't about perfection; it was about progress. And in the process, students began to see mistakes not as failures, but as stepping-stones to deeper understanding.

The simple task of getting students to correct mistakes and explain their reasoning invites them into a deeper level of thinking. Of course, getting the right answer is important. But when students explain the process they used to arrive at an answer, teachers gain valuable insight into their understanding. As Carnegie Learning points out, right answers show what a student *got*, but the reasoning shows what they *know*.[3] It's through these explanations that teachers can better assess both strengths and areas for growth.

When students take the time to reflect on their reasoning, they naturally build their metacognitive skills. They begin to recognize patterns in their thinking, develop stronger problem-solving strategies, and ultimately become more confident learners. Research by Glass and Maher supports this, noting that the act of explaining and justifying prompts students to engage in sense-making and meaningful reflection.[4] Simply put, this reasoning and reflection turns thinking into learning.

As students begin to use reflection to identify their own learning challenges, plan solutions, take action, and reflect on those actions, they become more aware of their thinking processes and decision-making. This encourages them to notice what strategies work well for them and where they might need to adjust. Over time, this practice helps students grow into self-aware learners who can advocate for themselves and make thoughtful choices about their learning. They begin to see that growth isn't just something that happens, it's something they can actively create.

Cognitive Coaching®, developed by Costa and Garmston, emphasizes reflective dialogue and thought-provoking questions to help educators think more deeply about their practice.[5] Allyson studied Cognitive Coaching with a remarkable educational leader named Carolyn McKanders, who once said something she'll never forget: "No learning is complete until reflection has taken place."

The reality is, we do not offer students enough structured opportunities to reflect on their learning. Action Research is a way to change that. As they engage in cycles of inquiry, students build the mindset and habits of reflective, self-directed learners, all while gaining insight not only into what they learn but how they learn it.

Action Research for Students

Let's step into a science class where students are preparing for their first big unit test. In this classroom, rather than assigning a traditional study guide, the teacher invited students to take a different approach. She introduced Action Research as a way to explore how they learn best. She asked the students to reflect on their learning in that unit, thinking through the successes and challenges they had. She then asked them to get curious and come up with a question about how they can better prepare for the unit test.

Each student started with a personal question. One thoughtful and quiet student asked himself, "What's the best way for me to remember the key terms?" He had tried flashcards before but wasn't sure they worked. He wanted to test other strategies to see what actually helped the content stick.

The teacher then asked students to plan a strategy to address the challenge. In this planning phase, the student decided to try three different methods over the course of the week. He decided on drawing concept maps, teaching the material to a friend, and using an online flashcard app.

With the teacher's guidance on how to track his progress, he decided that each day he would rate how confident he felt with the terms, noting which method he used, tracking how much time he spent and how well he remembered the content the next day. As the student collected data, something surprising emerged—he found that drawing concept maps helped him *see* how ideas were connected, which made it easier to recall them later. Teaching the material was fun, but sometimes he got off track. Flashcards worked okay, but only if he used them consistently.

In the final stage, the student reflected on what he learned. He created a one-page summary of his process and shared it in a small group. He told his classmates, "I used to study without thinking about what worked best. Now, I know I learn better when I can organize ideas visually." Through this small inquiry, this student became more aware of himself as a learner. He discovered a better study method, but even more importantly he built the habit of *thinking about his thinking*.

As students practice and become better at using the process of Action Research, they take on the role of active investigators of their own growth. Just like teachers, students can use the steps of Action Research to explore, question, and reflect on their experiences. This approach builds academic skills, *and* it fosters deeper awareness of how they think and learn. In order to teach students how to start thinking and reflecting on their own learning, teachers will need to clearly explain the steps and model with examples. Depending on the grade level of students, they may even try a whole-class example first. By guiding students through a cycle of curiosity, planning, experimenting, and reflecting, we give them the tools to develop strong metacognitive habits. The result? Students who are more self-aware, more resilient, and more engaged in their journey as learners. The following framework offers a way to integrate Action Research into the classroom. These steps will support students in becoming more thoughtful, reflective problem-solvers in and beyond the classroom.

Student-Friendly Action Research Cycle

To support students as they begin using Action Research, teachers can guide them through a simple, repeatable cycle rooted in metacognition. These steps can be introduced one at a time, modeled with examples, and adapted by age group. As students gain confidence, they begin to own the process and apply it independently.

Step 1: Start with Curiosity: Identifying a Question

Metacognition begins with awareness, and Action Research starts with a question. Invite students to notice something about their learning that feels challenging or intriguing. Maybe it's "Why do I forget vocabulary words so quickly?" or "What helps me stay focused during reading time?" Framing their own learning questions encourages students to tune into how they learn and not just what they learn.[6]

Step 2: Plan and Experiment: Testing Strategies

Once students have a question, help them brainstorm strategies they could try. Maybe they'll set a goal to reread their notes nightly, use a new study method, or ask more questions during class discussions. Here, metacognition kicks in as students think about *how* they're learning and why certain strategies might work better for them.

Step 3: Monitor and Reflect: Gathering Data

Students begin observing themselves as learners by taking notes, journaling, or using checklists to track their progress. As they monitor their thinking, they can begin to notice patterns such as when they feel most confident, what strategies help them push through confusion, or when they tend to give up. This self-awareness is the heart of metacognition.

Step 4: Analyze and Adjust: Learning from Reflection

At the end of the cycle of inquiry, students review what happened. What worked? What didn't? Why? This stage is packed with reflection. They go beyond just reporting outcomes to interpreting their experience. This reflection deepens metacognition because students begin making connections between their actions and results. They learn how to pivot, adjust, and grow. John Dewey is often credited with reminding us that we do not learn from our experiences, we learn from reflecting on our experiences.[7]

Step 5: Share and Celebrate: Building a Culture of Reflection

Have students present their findings through mini-conferences, posters, gallery walks, or class discussions. Sharing not only builds confidence, it normalizes reflection and mistake-making. Students learn from each other and realize that being aware of their thinking is a skill they can practice.

An example completed by students might look like this:

Step 1: Identify a Learning Challenge What's something you're struggling with or want to understand better? *Examples: "I forget what I read," "I rush through math," "I get nervous before presentations."*	I forget what I read, especially when I have to remember it later for a quiz or class discussion. I want to remember the key points from what I read so I can talk about it in class and do better on quizzes.
Step 2: Choose a Strategy to Try What new approach or strategy will you try to help you improve? When and where will you use it? For how long will you try this strategy? *Examples: rereading, graphic organizers, taking breaks, peer feedback, self-quizzing, etc.* Strategy I will try: Time/place: I will use this strategy for: ___ days/weeks.	I will use sticky notes to write down the main idea of each paragraph as I read, then summarize the whole chapter in my own words at the end. I will use this strategy for two weeks during silent reading time in language arts and at home when I read my social studies textbook.

Step 3: Collect Evidence and Analyze Results What did you do? When did you do it? What did you notice?	Date	What I Tried	What I Remembered
	Apr 1	Sticky notes + summary	A few main ideas
	Apr 3	Sticky notes + summary	Most of the info
	Apr 5	Sticky notes only	Not much
	Apr 8	Sticky notes + summary + reread	Almost everything
Step 4: Reflect on the Results What worked? What would you do differently next time?	I remembered more when I used both sticky notes and a full summary. On days I skipped the summary, I didn't retain as much. Rereading also helped. I learned that writing in my own words and reviewing later helps me understand and remember better. I will keep using this strategy and add rereading when I have time.		

By embedding metacognition in the Action Research cycle, students become researchers of their own minds. They build the habits of asking questions, trying new strategies, monitoring their progress, and reflecting with purpose. It's not just about becoming better students, it's about becoming reflective, lifelong learners.

Combining curiosity, reflection, and intentional strategy, Action Research becomes a vehicle for both instruction and transformation. It helps students see that learning isn't just something that happens to them, it's something they can shape. As teachers model the process and guide students through cycles of inquiry, students learn to trust their questions, reflect on their experiences, and take meaningful steps toward growth. In the end, Action Research is more than just a tool for improvement: it's a mindset that builds confident, capable, and self-directed learners, ready to take on challenges in school and in life.

KEY QUESTIONS TO MOVE FROM TALK INTO ACTION

1. How might Action Research deepen your students' understanding of how they learn best?
2. In what ways can you intentionally model and scaffold metacognitive thinking in your classroom?
3. What structures or routines can you implement to support students in using reflection as a regular part of their learning process?

CONCLUSION

Collective Hope

When We Believe in Each Other, Everything Changes

> *Placing hope at the core of our school community provides encouragement and promotes clear thinking and informed action, giving us the leverage we need to close the achievement gap and solve other intractable problems.*
>
> —THOMAS J. SERGIOVANNI

Not too long ago, Allyson stepped into a second-grade team meeting, not sure what to expect. She was pleasantly surprised and smiled as she saw the teachers gathered around the table perusing a new set of phonics data. Just a few months earlier, these same teachers had been very discouraged, almost to the point of defeat. At the start of the school year, the team had assessed their students' reading skills, and the results were disheartening. The gap between where students were and where they needed to be was significant, and the idea of closing that distance felt overwhelming. This team was known for producing strong results, and they'd cautioned Allyson not to expect the usual growth this time around. "We've never had a group come in this far behind," one teacher had said, her voice heavy with worry.

But today was different.

As Allyson approached the table, she immediately felt a shift in energy. The room was filled with pride and joy rather than with anxiety.

One of the teachers leaned forward with a wide grin and said, "You're not going to believe this, but they did it!" Another chimed in, "They've all mastered the phonemic awareness skills we were so worried about at the beginning of the year!" Heads nodded all around the table, eyes bright with celebration. Allyson couldn't help but join their excitement. The teachers went on to share that their students had caught up in foundational reading skills, and now many were now performing at or near grade level. It was a huge turnaround, and the sense of accomplishment was more than evident.

You see, when we looked at these same students as numbers on a fall data chart, they didn't look like high achievers. But what the data didn't show was the intentional instruction and constant progress monitoring this team had poured into their work. They used common formative assessments as a way to analyze their understanding of concepts and skills, noting the students' strengths even when they were significantly below grade level. The teachers knew what specific skills the students needed to develop next. They made instructional decisions based on real-time learning, not just pacing guides. They met often, shared strategies, and asked each other, "What worked for your group? What might I try with mine?"

This wasn't by chance. It was the result of meaningful collaboration, high expectations, and a whole lot of heart. It was the magic that happens when educators believe in the power of growth and use every strategy or tool they can to help students get there. It is what happens when teachers have a deep-held belief that what they do in the classroom with students makes a difference. In other words, these teachers had both self-efficacy and collective efficacy.

Self-efficacy is the belief in our own ability to achieve goals and improve outcomes. Another word for self-efficacy is "hope." Hope is not wishing on a star that things will change. Hope is the fire inside of you, even if it is just an ember, that helps you tackle challenges and look forward to the future. Hope doesn't mean that we ignore reality, it means that we face reality with a fierce belief that we have the power to make it better. Hope is often lacking as we look at the challenges we face in schools. Yet hope can ignite a fire that leads to action plans that lead to dramatic, empowering change. When educators engage in Action Research, they can immediately see the impact of the practices they put into place. The same is true for students. Rather than focusing on task completion, they focus on incremental steps that result in achieving goals.

Action Research empowers you to write and tell the story of student learning and growth. The approaches to professional learning and collaboration we've explored in this book are intended to encourage you to try new things and to let student achievement lead the way to improve learning. The exciting part is that we can apply the same challenge-practice-results approach to all areas for improvement in schools and classrooms. When it becomes embedded in the school or district culture, educators and students embrace new ideas, take risks, and can change the face of education. Action Research creates a culture of "collective hope," where we know we can count on each other to set aside fears, learn from failure, and achieve more than we ever could alone.

Throughout this book, we've explored how powerful it is to focus on what's working rather than on only what's broken. We've seen that progress doesn't require perfection, but it does require belief. And belief, when paired with action, becomes transformation.

Now, we ask: Are you ready to talk less and act more? Are you ready to go on the exciting adventure that is Action Research? Are you ready and willing to dive into shared goals and become the transformative team your students deserve? And are you ready to help your students experience that same kind of transformation?

Let's build schools where hope is more than a feeling. Let's make it the outcome of our beliefs, our systems, and our shared commitment to students. Hope grows where efficacy lives. When we believe in ourselves and each other, there's no limit to what our students can achieve.

Endnotes

Introduction

1. Kobi Yamada, *What Do You Do with a Problem?*, illus. Mae Besom (Compendium, 2016).
2. Kobi Yamada, *What Do You Do with an Idea?*, illus. Mae Besom (Compendium, 2014).
3. Kobi Yamada, *What Do You Do with a Chance?*, illus. Mae Besom (Compendium, 2018).
4. Clifford Adelman, "Kurt Lewin and the Origins of Action Research," *Educational Action Research* 1, no. 1 (1993): 7–24, accessed April 13, 2025, https://doi.org/10.1080/0965079930010102.

Chapter 1

1. Lida Colbert, "Beliefs and Behaviors—What You Need to Know to Make Change Possible," *Chris Kolenda Blog*, March 21, 2022, accessed April 13, 2025, https://chriskolenda.com/beliefs-and-behaviors/; Katherine L. Milkman, *How to Change: The Science of Getting from Where You Are to Where You Want to Be*, foreword by Angela Duckworth (Portfolio/Penguin, 2021); Thomas R. Guskey, *Get Set, Go! Creating Successful Professional Learning for Results* (Corwin, 2020).
2. Guskey, *Get Set, Go!*
3. Khalil Smith, "Don't Change Beliefs, Change Behaviors," *Forbes*, August 11, 2019, accessed June 26, 2025, https://www.forbes.com/sites/khalilsmith/2019/08/11/dont-change-beliefs-change-behaviors/.
4. Douglas B. Reeves, *Fearless Grading: How to Improve Achievement, Discipline, and Culture through Accurate and Fair Grading* (Archway Publishing, 2023).
5. George Couros and Allyson Apsey, *What Makes a Great Principal: The Five Pillars of Effective School Leadership* (IMpress, 2024).
6. Brené Brown, *Daring Greatly: How the Courage to Be Vulnerable Transforms the Way We Live, Love, Parent, and Lead* (Gotham Books, 2012), 34.
7. Reeves, *Fearless Grading*.

Chapter 2

1. George Couros, *The Innovator's Mindset: Empower Learning, Unleash Talent, and Lead a Culture of Creativity* (Dave Burgess Consulting, 2015).

2. Timothy R. Clark, *The 4 Stages of Psychological Safety: Defining the Path to Inclusion and Innovation* (Berrett-Koehler Publishers, 2020), 11.

3. Clark, *The 4 Stages*, 12.

4. Sophie Barry, "The Future of Schools: Sir Ken Robinson Explains What 'Was Never True.'" School News Australia, 2018. Accessed June 26, 2025. https://www.school-news.com.au/news/the-future-of-schools-lies-in-questioning-s.

5. Reeves, *Fearless Grading*.

Chapter 5

1. Douglas B. Reeves, *From Leading to Succeeding: The Seven Elements of Effective Leadership* (Solution Tree Press, 2016), 47.

Chapter 7

1. John Hattie, *Visible Learning: The Sequel* (Routledge, 2023).

Chapter 8

1. Douglas B. Reeves, *Fearless Schools: Building Trust, Resilience, and Psychological Safety* (Archway Publishing, 2023).

2. FullStory, "Qualitative vs. Quantitative Data in Research: The Difference," *FullStory Blog*, accessed September 9, 2024, https://www.fullstory.com/blog/qualitative-vs-quantitative-data/.

Chapter 9

1. John Hattie, *Visible Learning for Teachers: Maximizing Impact on Learning* (Routledge, 2012), 8.

Chapter 10

1. Teresa M. Verland and Jodie L. Erickson, "Leading by Example: A Case Study of the Influence of Principal Self-Efficacy on Collective Efficacy," *Cogent Education* 4, no. 1 (2017): 1286765, accessed June 26, 2025, https://doi.org/10.1080/2331186X.2017.1286765.

2. John C. Maxwell, *The 21 Irrefutable Laws of Leadership*, 2nd ed. (Thomas Nelson, 2007), 161.

3. Kim Scott, *Radical Candor: Be a Kick-Ass Boss Without Losing Your Humanity*, revised and updated ed. (St. Martin's Press, 2019), 221.

4   Couros and Apsey, *What Makes a Great Principal*.

5   Couros and Apsey, *What Makes a Great Principal*, 80.

Chapter 11

1   John Hattie, *Visible Learning: The Sequel*. (Routledge, 2023) Rachel J. Eells, "Meta-Analysis of the Relationship between Collective Teacher Efficacy and Student Achievement," PhD diss., Loyola University Chicago, 2011, Accessed June 26, 2025. https://ecommons.luc.edu/cgi/viewcontent.cgi?article=1132&context=luc_diss.

2   Anita Williams Woolley, Ishani Aggarwal, and Thomas W. Malone, "Collective Intelligence in Teams and Organizations," In *The Handbook of Collective Intelligence*, edited by Thomas W. Malone and Michael S. Bernstein, (MIT Press, 2015), 143-167.

3   Creative Leadership Solutions, *Fearless Instruction: High-Impact Strategies Inspired by 90/90/90 Schools* (Creative Leadership Press, 2025).

Chapter 12

1   Sarah Weitzman and Rachel Feirson, "Implementing the Stripling Model for Student-Led Inquiry," *Edutopia*, accessed June 26, 2025, https://www.edutopia.org/article/teaching-stripling-model-inquiry-middle-school/.

2   Nathaniel Saaris, "Mastering Metacognition: The What, Why, and How." *Actively Learn Blog*, February 23, 2017, accessed April 13, 2025, https://www.activelylearn.com/post/metacognition.

3   Carnegie Learning, "Facilitating Discourse," Carnegie Learning Help Center. Accessed September 7, 2025, https://www.carnegielearning.com/texas-help/article/facilitating-discourse/.

4   Barbara Glass and Carolyn A. Maher, "Students' Problem Solving and Justification, in *Proceedings of the 28th Conference of the International Group for the Psychology of Mathematics Education* (PME 28), vol. 2, 463–70. 2004.

5   Arthur L. Costa and Robert J. Garmston, *Cognitive Coaching: Developing Self-Directed Leaders and Learners*, 3rd ed. (Rowman & Littlefield, 2016).

6   Warren Berger, *A More Beautiful Question: The Power of Inquiry to Spark Breakthrough Ideas* (Bloomsbury USA, 2016).

7   Tom McKenzie, "A Crucial Component of Learning." *Institute for Excell*.

Acknowledgments

To Dr. Douglas Reeves, whose vision lights the way.

To Lisa Almeida, whose leadership lifts others higher.

To Dave Burgess and the team at DBC for helping educators help each other.

To the educators who dare to act. Your courage and commitment are the heartbeat of this book.

And to our families, our constant light and greatest joy.

About Allyson Apsey and Emily Freeland

Allyson Apsey has been an award-winning school leader for nearly twenty years, leading all levels from elementary to high school after teaching elementary and middle school students. She is the author of several books, including the best sellers *What Makes a Great Principal*, *Lead with Collaboration*, *Leading the Whole Teacher*, and *The Path to Serendipity*. Her greatest joy comes from working with dedicated groups of educators to support them in taking care of the whole child and the whole educator by implementing research-proven practices. Allyson's TEDx Talk can give you an insight into her passion. She currently serves districts, schools, and organizations throughout the country as a keynote speaker, professional learning provider, and instruction and leadership coach. Connect with her on social media at @AllysonApsey or visit her website at allysonapsey.com.

Dr. Emily Freeland has over thirty-two years of experience that includes administrative positions at the state, district, and school levels, as well as teaching science. Much of her work has been concentrated in schools that were identified as underperforming and targeted the implementation of school turnaround principles, the effective use of data, closing  achievement gaps, and increasing graduation rates. She currently serves districts and schools across the nation as an instruction and leadership coach. Emily's book, *From Ghost to Graduates: An Educator's Guide to Identifying and Reconnecting Disengaged Students*, highlights her expertise as a certified National Dropout Prevention Specialist and focuses on strategies that address the causes of disengagement, including the context of pandemic learning and its impact on students who were previously not at risk of dropping out.

Bring Allyson and Emily to Your District, School or Event

If the ideas in this book inspired you, imagine the impact of bringing them to life with your team. Allyson Apsey and Emily Freeland partner with schools and districts across the country to provide professional development, facilitate Action Research, and offer coaching that moves educators from conversation to meaningful results.

We would be honored to support your district, school, or event. To learn more or to schedule, connect with us at allysonapsey@gmail.com or ekfreeland@gmail.com.

You can also visit www.allysonapsey.com or www.creativeleadership.net for more information.

Please check out Allyson and Emily's other books:

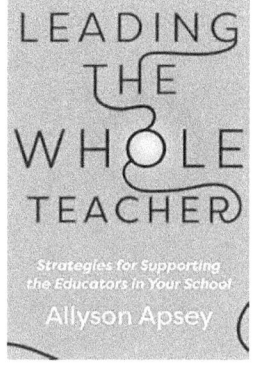

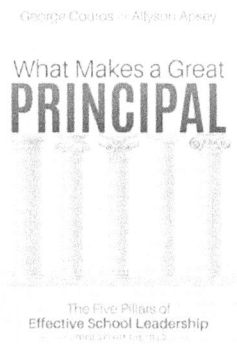

More from Dave Burgess Consulting, Inc.

Since 2012, DBCI has published books that inspire and equip educators to be their best. For more information on our titles or to purchase bulk orders for your school, district, or book study, visit DaveBurgessConsulting.com/DBCIbooks.

The *Like a PIRATE*™ Series

Teach Like a PIRATE by Dave Burgess

Balance Like a PIRATE by Jessica Cabeen, Jessica Johnson, and Sarah Johnson

eXPlore Like a PIRATE by Michael Matera

Learn Like a PIRATE by Paul Solarz

Plan Like a PIRATE by Dawn M. Harris

Play Like a PIRATE by Quinn Rollins

Run Like a PIRATE by Adam Welcome

Tech Like a PIRATE by Matt Miller

The *Lead Like a PIRATE*™ Series

Lead Like a PIRATE by Shelley Burgess and Beth Houf

Lead Beyond Your Title by Nili Bartley

Lead with Appreciation by Amber Teamann and Melinda Miller

Lead with Collaboration by Allyson Apsey and Jessica Gomez

Lead with Culture by Jay Billy

Lead with Instructional Rounds by Vicki Wilson

Lead with Literacy by Mandy Ellis

She Leads by Dr. Rachael George and Majalise W. Tolan

The EduProtocol Field Guide Series

Deploying EduProtocols by Kim Voge, with Jon Corippo and Marlena Hebern

The EduProtocol Field Guide by Marlena Hebern and Jon Corippo

The EduProtocol Field Guide Book 2 by Marlena Hebern and Jon Corippo

The EduProtocol Field Guide ELA Edition by Jacob Carr

The EduProtocol Field Guide Math Edition by Lisa Nowakowski and Jeremiah Ruesch

The EduProtocol Field Guide Primary Edition by Benjamin Cogswell and Jennifer Dean

The EduProtocol Field Guide Social Studies Edition by Dr. Scott M. Petri and Adam Moler

Leadership & School Culture

Be 1% Better by Ron Clark

Be THAT Teacher by Dwayne Reed

Beyond the Surface of Restorative Practices by Marisol Rerucha

Change the Narrative by Henry J. Turner and Kathy Lopes

Choosing to See by Pamela Seda and Kyndall Brown

Culturize by Jimmy Casas

Discipline Win by Andy Jacks

Educate Me! by Dr. Shree Walker with Micheal D. Ison

Escaping the School Leader's Dunk Tank by Rebecca Coda and Rick Jetter

Fight Song by Kim Bearden

From Teacher to Leader by Starr Sackstein

If the Dance Floor Is Empty, Change the Song by Joe Clark

The Innovator's Mindset by George Couros

It's OK to Say "They" by Christy Whittlesey

Kids Deserve It! by Todd Nesloney and Adam Welcome

Leading the Whole Teacher by Allyson Apsey

Let Them Speak by Rebecca Coda and Rick Jetter

The Limitless School by Abe Hege and Adam Dovico

Live Your Excellence by Jimmy Casas

Next-Level Teaching by Jonathan Alsheimer

The Pepper Effect by Sean Gaillard

Principaled by Kate Barker, Kourtney Ferrua, and Rachael George

The Principled Principal by Jeffrey Zoul and Anthony McConnell

Relentless by Hamish Brewer

The Secret Solution by Todd Whitaker, Sam Miller, and Ryan Donlan

Start. Right. Now. by Todd Whitaker, Jeffrey Zoul, and Jimmy Casas

Stop. Right. Now. by Jimmy Casas and Jeffrey Zoul

Teach Your Class Off by CJ Reynolds

Teachers Deserve It by Rae Hughart and Adam Welcome

They Call Me "Mr. De" by Frank DeAngelis

Thrive Through the Five by Jill M. Siler

Unmapped Potential by Julie Hasson and Missy Lennard

When Kids Lead by Todd Nesloney and Adam Dovico

Word Shift by Joy Kirr

Your School Rocks by Ryan McLane and Eric Lowe

MORE FROM DAVE BURGESS CONSULTING, INC.

Technology & Tools

50 Things to Go Further with Google Classroom by Alice Keeler and Libbi Miller

50 Things You Can Do with Google Classroom by Alice Keeler and Libbi Miller

50 Ways to Engage Students with Google Apps by Alice Keeler and Heather Lyon

140 Twitter Tips for Educators by Brad Currie, Billy Krakower, and Scott Rocco

AI Optimism by Becky Keene

Block Breaker by Brian Aspinall

Building Blocks for Tiny Techies by Jamila "Mia" Leonard

Code Breaker by Brian Aspinall

The Complete EdTech Coach by Katherine Goyette and Adam Juarez

Control Alt Achieve by Eric Curts

The Esports Education Playbook by Chris Aviles, Steve Isaacs, Christine Lion-Bailey, and Jesse Lubinsky

Google Apps for Littles by Christine Pinto and Alice Keeler

Master the Media by Julie Smith

Raising Digital Leaders by Jennifer Casa-Todd

Reality Bytes by Christine Lion-Bailey, Jesse Lubinsky, and Micah Shippee, PhD

Sail the 7 Cs with Microsoft Education by Becky Keene and Kathi Kersznowski

Shake Up Learning by Kasey Bell

Social LEADia by Jennifer Casa-Todd

Stepping Up to Google Classroom by Alice Keeler and Kimberly Mattina

Teaching Math with Google Apps by Alice Keeler and Diana Herrington

Teaching with Google Jamboard by Alice Keeler and Kimberly Mattina

Teachingland by Amanda Fox and Mary Ellen Weeks

Teaching Methods & Materials

All 4s and 5s by Andrew Sharos

Boredom Busters by Katie Powell

Building Strong Writers by Christina Schneider

The Classroom Chef by John Stevens and Matt Vaudrey

The Collaborative Classroom by Trevor Muir

Copyrighteous by Diana Gill

CREATE by Bethany J. Petty

Ditch That Homework by Matt Miller and Alice Keeler

Ditch That Textbook by Matt Miller

Don't Ditch That Tech by Matt Miller, Nate Ridgway, and Angelia Ridgway

EDrenaline Rush by John Meehan

Educated by Design by Michael Cohen, The Tech Rabbi

Empowered to Choose: A Practical Guide to Personalized Learning by Andrew Easton

Expedition Science by Becky Schnekser

Frustration Busters by Katie Powell

Fully Engaged by Michael Matera and John Meehan

Game On? Brain On! by Lindsay Portnoy, PhD

Guided Math AMPED by Reagan Tunstall

Happy & Resilient by Roni Habib

Innovating Play by Jessica LaBar-Twomy and Christine Pinto

Instant Relevance by Denis Sheeran

Instructional Coaching Connection by Nathan Lang-Raad

Keeping the Wonder by Jenna Copper, Ashley Bible, Abby Gross, and Staci Lamb

MORE FROM DAVE BURGESS CONSULTING, INC.

LAUNCH by John Spencer and A.J. Juliani

Learning in the Zone by Dr. Sonny Magana

Lights, Cameras, TEACH! by Kevin J. Butler

Make Learning MAGICAL by Tisha Richmond

Pass the Baton by Kathryn Finch and Theresa Hoover

Project-Based Learning Anywhere by Lori Elliott

Pure Genius by Don Wettrick

The Revolution by Darren Ellwein and Derek McCoy

The Science Box by Kim Adsit and Adam Peterson

Shift This! by Joy Kirr

Skyrocket Your Teacher Coaching by Michael Cary Sonbert

Spark Learning by Ramsey Musallam

Sparks in the Dark by Travis Crowder and Todd Nesloney

Table Talk Math by John Stevens

Teachables by Cheryl Abla and Lisa Maxfield

Unpack Your Impact by Naomi O'Brien and LaNesha Tabb

The Wild Card by Hope and Wade King

Writefully Empowered by Jacob Chastain

The Writing on the Classroom Wall by Steve Wyborney

You Are Poetry by Mike Johnston

You'll Never Guess What I'm Saying by Naomi O'Brien

You'll Never Guess What I'm Thinking About by Naomi O'Brien

Inspiration, Professional Growth & Personal Development

Be REAL by Tara Martin

Be the One for Kids by Ryan Sheehy

The Coach ADVenture by Amy Illingworth

Creatively Productive by Lisa Johnson

The Ed Branding Book by Dr. Renae Bryant and Lynette White

Educational Eye Exam by Alicia Ray

The EduNinja Mindset by Jennifer Burdis

Empower Our Girls by Lynmara Colón and Adam Welcome

Finding Lifelines by Andrew Grieve and Andrew Sharos

The Four O'Clock Faculty by Rich Czyz

How Much Water Do We Have? by Pete and Kris Nunweiler

P Is for Pirate by Dave and Shelley Burgess

A Passion for Kindness by Tamara Letter

The Path to Serendipity by Allyson Apsey

PheMOMenal Teacher by Annick Rauch

Recipes for Resilience by Robert A. Martinez

Rogue Leader by Rich Czyz

Sanctuaries by Dan Tricarico

Saving Sycamore by Molly B. Hudgens

The Secret Sauce by Rich Czyz

Shattering the Perfect Teacher Myth by Aaron Hogan

Stories from Webb by Todd Nesloney

Talk to Me by Kim Bearden

Teach Better by Chad Ostrowski, Tiffany Ott, Rae Hughart, and Jeff Gargas

Teach Me, Teacher by Jacob Chastain

Teach, Play, Learn! by Adam Peterson

Teaching Is a Tattoo by Mike Johnston

The Teachers of Oz by Herbie Raad and Nathan Lang-Raad

Teaching the Ms. Abbott Way by Joyce Stephens Abbott

TeamMakers by Laura Robb and Evan Robb

Through the Lens of Serendipity by Allyson Apsey

Write Here and Now by Dan Tricarico

The Zen Teacher by Dan Tricarico

Children's Books

The Adventures of Little Mickey by Mickey Smith Jr.

Alpert by LaNesha Tabb

Alpert & Friends by LaNesha Tabb

Beyond Us by Aaron Polansky

Cannonball In by Tara Martin

Dolphins in Trees by Aaron Polansky

Dragon Smart by Tisha and Tommy Richmond

I Can Achieve Anything by MoNique Waters

I Want to Be a Lot by Ashley Savage

The Magic of Wonder by Jenna Copper, Ashley Bible, Abby Gross, and Staci Lamb

Micah's Big Question by Naomi O'Brien

The Princes of Serendip by Allyson Apsey

Ride with Emilio by Richard Nares

A Teacher's Top Secret Confidential by LaNesha Tabb

A Teacher's Top Secret: Mission Accomplished by LaNesha Tabb

The Wild Card Kids by Hope and Wade King

Zom-Be a Design Thinker by Amanda Fox

www.ingramcontent.com/pod-product-compliance
Lightning Source LLC
Chambersburg PA
CBHW050554160426
43199CB00015B/2656